D1278099

THE SCOPES
MONKEYTRIAL

MILESTONES
IN AMERICAN HISTORY

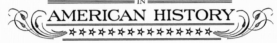

THE SCOPES MONKEY TRIAL

SAMUEL WILLARD CROMPTON

CHELSEA HOUSE
PUBLISHERS
An imprint of Infobase Publishing

The Scopes Monkey Trial

Copyright © 2010 by Infobase Publishing

All rights reserved. No part of this book may be reproduced or utilized in any form or by any means, electronic or mechanical, including photocopying, recording, or by any information storage or retrieval systems, without permission in writing from the publisher. For information, contact:

Chelsea House
An imprint of Infobase Publishing
132 West 31st Street
New York, NY 10001

Library of Congress Cataloging-in-Publication Data

Crompton, Samuel Willard.
The Scopes monkey trial : the debate over evolution/ Samuel Willard Crompton.
  p. cm.—(Milestones in American history)
Includes bibliographical references and index.
ISBN 978-1-60413-679-1 (hardcover)
1. Scopes, John Thomas—Trials, litigation, etc.—Juvenile literature. 2. Evolution (Biol-ogy)—Study and teaching—Law and legislation—Tennessee—Juvenile literature. I. Title.
II. Series.
KF224.S3C76 2010
345.73'0288—dc22   2009029615

Chelsea House books are available at special discounts when purchased in bulk quantities for businesses, associations, institutions, or sales promotions. Please call our Special Sales Department in New York at (212) 967-8800 or (800) 322-8755.

You can find Chelsea House on the World Wide Web at http://www.chelseahouse.com

Text design by Erik Lindstrom
Cover design by Alicia Post
Composition by Keith Trego
Cover printed by Bang Printing, Brainerd, MN
Book printed and bound by Bang Printing, Brainerd, MN
Date printed: January 2010
Printed in the United States of America

10 9 8 7 6 5 4 3 2 1

This book is printed on acid-free paper.

All links and Web addresses were checked and verified to be correct at the time of publication. Because of the dynamic nature of the Web, some addresses and links may have changed since publication and may no longer be valid.

CONTENTS

The Power
of Three

They were all troublemakers sitting in that Tennessee courtroom—from the old man wearing suspenders to the old man wearing a pith helmet to the middle-aged man wearing horn-rimmed spectacles.

The man with suspenders had made a fortune, and a national reputation, by taking cases that other lawyers shunned. He was a master at courtroom theatrics and at persuading juries to agree with him. If he turned surly, then nasty at times, well, it was all part of the performance.

The fellow who wore the pith helmet one day—and who fanned himself furiously during the trial—fancied himself the Great Commoner, the friend of the common man, but he had recently made a fortune in Florida real estate. More important, he had the habit of fastening onto causes that advanced his reputation, whether they were in the public interest or not.

As for the man with the horn-rimmed glasses, he was by far the worst of the bunch. A man of tremendous literary talent, possessing one of the finest pens ever known in American literature, he had descended to the rank of cynic and critic: choosing to label just about anyone and anything as hopeless, backward, and corrupt.

All three men were sincere. One can argue that they were so thoroughly themselves that they could not help acting the parts they did. Those who knew them best admired their finer aspects and raised their eyes in hopeless despair at some of their more ridiculous antics.

Clarence Darrow, William Jennings Bryan, and H.L. Mencken were about to make history in the Scopes Monkey Trial of July 1925.

THE DECADE

If the three men were unrepentant troublemakers, then the times were troubled, too. Americans of today often look back at the 1920s with nostalgia, admiring the automobiles and clothing. The Ford Motor Company was number one, turning out highly desired products, and high skirts and cigarettes were the rage. America was indeed in the "Jazz Age," and Americans were having their fill of the first movies (which were all silent until 1927), automobile rides, and radio programs. But behind the scenes of exuberant joy lay a darker subtext: The 1920s were anything but harmonious. Americans had recently come through, or witnessed:

☆ The Great War (World War I), in which 130,000 men had laid down their lives,

☆ The Influenza Epidemic of 1918–1919, which had caused the deaths of more than 600,000 people,

☆ The Red Scare of 1919–1920, a time of strong anti-communism, which had made the future of civil liberties doubtful, and

☆ The resurgence in the size and power of the Ku Klux Klan, which now claimed that Catholics, Jews, and liberals were as undesirable as African Americans.

The 1920s were contentious times.

THE CONFLICT

At issue in the Tennessee courtroom was whether a person could teach evolution in the state's public schools. The state legislature had recently enacted a law that said that he could not.

At stake was the condition of public education in Tennessee, and perhaps elsewhere in the United States. Could school boards or state governments decide what parts of scientific knowledge should be excluded from the curriculum?

THE DEFENDANT

Twenty-four-year-old John T. Scopes was accused of violating Tennessee state law. He had as his defender Clarence Darrow, the greatest criminal attorney in the nation, who had prevailed in all sorts of unlikely situations. He had as his attacker the greatest orator of the past 100 years. Not since the golden days of Daniel Webster had America heard a speaker like William Jennings Bryan.

Scopes knew all about Bryan's illustrious, multifaceted career; in fact, he had lived for a time in Bryan's hometown. Scopes also knew plenty about the other man of distinction in the courtroom, Clarence Darrow. Although Scopes knew a great deal about the old ones (and they were old lions, full of fire and force), he did not know much about the middle-aged fellow, H.L. Mencken, who hailed from Baltimore to report on the case for the *Evening Sun*. In some ways, the journalist held

In 1925, John Scopes (1900–1970) became a willing participant in the ACLU's fight against the Butler Act. On May 5, he was charged with teaching evolution from a chapter from George Hunter's *Civic Biology*, a book that endorsed the theory of evolution. Thus began one of the most famous trials of the century, the Scopes Monkey Trial.

the balance of power in the situation, for millions of Americans would hear about the Scopes Monkey Trial from his pen.

The proceedings began, and as they say, America has never been the same.

From Darwin to Dayton

Evolution, as a subject of debate, had only been around for 65 years when the Scopes Trial began. Evolution, or more properly, the theory of natural selection, had come to light in the autumn of 1859, with the publication of *The Origin of Species*.

THE MAN

Charles Darwin (1809–1882) was a proper Victorian gentleman who had studied at the University of Edinburgh, then taken his degree from Cambridge University. Born on precisely the same day as Abraham Lincoln, February 12, Darwin was, by 1859, a comfortable, prosperous man, surrounded by a happy family; his children were the apples of his eye. But in the recesses of his study, Darwin had been troubled for years by the data he had amassed and the disturbing conclusions to which he had reluctantly come.

HIS THEORY

Darwin had spent five years aboard the HMS *Beagle*, a British survey ship, as an unofficial natural scientist. During the voyages that took him around the Southern Hemisphere, Darwin had noticed slight variations between animals of the same species, sometimes when they lived on islands only two miles (three kilometers) apart. Returning to England in 1838, Darwin had catalogued his specimens and continued to do research into the variations he found. By 1859, he was ready to release his findings to the world. Through more than 20 years of painstaking research, he found that:

☆ Slight variations happened naturally.
☆ Those variations gave rise to some animals that were "more fit" to survive and others that were not.
☆ The more "fit" animals tended to pass their variations on to the next generation.

If Darwin had stopped here, leaving his readers to draw their own conclusions, *The Origin of Species* might not have been controversial. He went a full step further, however, saying that:

☆ Species were *mutable*; they changed over time.

Mutable was a dangerous word. Many, if not most, Victorians of Darwin's time believed that species were *immutable*, meaning that Earth and its creatures were, in 1859, very much as God had made them. According to the calculations of a prominent seventeenth-century bishop, the world was only about 6,000 years old.

Darwin was a religious man; in fact, he had once considered becoming a minister in the Anglican (Church of England) faith. Yet, his conclusions led him, and many who read his works, in a very different direction. To anyone who accepted the idea of natural selection (the word *evolution* was not used yet), it was

Charles Darwin's *The Origin of Species*, which was published in 1859, proposed that life evolved by natural selection over millions of years. Still, he avoided mentioning the word *evolution*. Darwin's second book, *The Descent of Man* (1871), directly addressed the debate over the origin of humankind, arguing that "man is descended from a hairy, tailed quadruped, probably arboreal in its habits."

apparent that Earth had to be more than 6,000 years old. The variations between animals were so distinct that they had to have "evolved" over a long period of time. And so Darwin became a free-thinking scientist even though it pained him to do so.

THE FIRESTORM

Controversy swirled around *The Origin of Species*, almost from the day of its publication. The educated public in Victorian Britain quickly divided into two camps: those who reluctantly accepted the new scientific theory, and those who adamantly opposed it. A series of debates were held, with the biologist T.H. Huxley speaking for natural selection and Samuel Wilberforce (a prominent churchman and the grandson of the man who had led the movement to abolish slavery in England) speaking against it. Because there was no radio in 1860, people went to hear the debates. Most came away believing that Huxley had done better and that natural selection was on its way to becoming an established part of science. If Darwin had stopped there, his controversial theory might have slipped under some of the trip wires set by its opponents, but, as a person of science, he felt compelled to reveal all that he knew. In 1871, he published *The Descent of Man*.

APES AND CHIMPANZEES!

If *The Origin of Species* had been controversial, then *The Descent of Man* was spectacularly so. Darwin again employed a great mass of research, and great skill with his pen (he wrote compelling prose), to demonstrate a theory. This time, he declared that humans were rather closely related to apes and chimpanzees. In other words, men and women were not the most special part of creation. Instead they were the latest, most recent stage of an evolutionary tree that went all the way back to the single-celled protozoa.

Many Victorian Englishmen and women had been able to accept the idea that species were mutable, but to say that they were either the descendants of or related to apes and chimpanzees was, for them, an enormous stretch. Here they had been raised, in the Church of England, on the idea that humans were special, the epitome of God's creation, and now Darwin was telling them that they were nothing more than the product of evolutionary changes and variations. Darwin, anticipating the trouble that *The Descent of Man* would create, tried to forestall it with these words, on the last page of the book:

> The main conclusion arrived at in this work, namely, that man is descended from some lowly organized form, will, I regret to think, be highly distasteful to many. But there can hardly be a doubt that we are descended from barbarians. The astonishment which I felt on first seeing a party of Fuegians [from Tierra del Fuego] on a wild and broken shore will never be forgotten by me, for the reflection at once raced into my mind—such were our ancestors. These men were absolutely naked and bedaubed with paint, their long hair was tangled, their mouths frothed with excitement, and their expression was wild, startled, and distrustful. They possessed hardly any arts, and like wild animals lived on what they could catch; they had no government, and were merciless to every one not of their own small tribe.[1]

Darwin went on to write that he could not be proud of such people as representative of his ancestors and that he might even prefer to be descended from, or related to, apes and chimpanzees:

> For my own part I would as soon be descended from that heroic little monkey, who braved his dreaded enemy in order to save the life of his keeper, or from that old baboon, who descending from the mountains, carried away in triumph his young comrade from a crowd of astonished dogs—as from a savage who delights to torture his enemies, offers up bloody

sacrifices, practices infanticide without remorse, treats his wives like slaves, knows no decency, and is haunted by the grossest superstitions.[2]

Even as Darwin tried to soften the blow, he threw in one last sentence (the last of the book) that had to haunt many of his readers: "Man still bears in his bodily frame the indelible stamp of his lowly origin."[3]

ACROSS THE OCEAN

When Darwin died in 1882, his body was interred at Westminster Abbey, where England honors its greatest sons and daughters. As unappealing as his two key theories were (natural selection and man's place in the evolutionary tree), a majority of the educated public had come to accept them. Even if one disagreed with Darwin, or hated the conclusions to which he had come, one had to admire his painstaking accumulation of evidence: here was a true person of science.

That view was not shared on the western side of the Atlantic.

Part of the reason was national prejudice. Though Americans and Britons had stopped fighting on the battlefield (the last time was in 1815 at the Battle of New Orleans), the two peoples still viewed each other with some suspicion. This was especially true at the less educated levels of society. That an Englishman had come to this theory (natural selection and the descent of man started to be fused into the word *evolution*) rested ill with many Americans; that they were descended from or related to apes and chimpanzees was both disturbing and hilarious. Many clubs and organizations claimed to spend time searching for the "missing link" between humans and apes.

Even so, well-educated Americans tended to accept Darwin's theories, and by 1880, a marked split was noticed. Those who went to the best colleges and universities tended to believe in evolution—even if they did not like it—and those who had only a primary education either did not believe in the theory

Pictured is a fossil cast of "Ida," a 47-million-year-old fossil at London's Natural History Museum in May 2009. Also known as *Darwinius masillae*, Ida was discovered in Germany by a team of Norwegian scientists and is thought to be the evolutionary "missing link" between humans and our distant ancestors.

or had never heard of it. This state of affairs changed soon after the beginning of the new century, in which the number of high schools and high school students increased exponentially.

NEW BOOKS

Until about 1910, the majority of public-school textbooks were of rather poor quality. Many had not changed their scientific

WILLIAM GRAHAM SUMNER

*"There are no rights. The world owes nobody a living."**

This answer came from one of Yale University's most distinguished professors and, perhaps, the single most popular professor Yale has ever had.

Born in New Jersey in 1840, William Graham Sumner earned his bachelor's degree from Yale, studied in Germany for two years, and then returned to the life of the academic in America. He became a full professor of political and social science in 1872. For the rest of his long career, he drew undergraduates in a way that was unmatched in his own time and has seldom been equaled since.

Familiar with Darwinism from his time in Germany, Sumner became the leading exponent of what has ever since been called social Darwinism. This means that competition among individuals drives social evolution in human societies. Those with the most economic, physical, or technological power will survive and outlive the weak. The context of the above quotation, which comes from the pen of one of Sumner's students, is as follows:

"Professor, don't you believe in any government aid to industries?

"No! It's root, hog, or die.

"Yes, but hasn't the hog got a right to root?

data for a generation or more. One goal of the Progressive Movement (a movement for reform favoring social and economic equality that flourished from 1900 to 1920) was the improvement of schools and textbooks, and George William Hunter's *A Civic Biology: Presented in Problems* was one of the new crop.

A high school teacher in New York City, Hunter conferred with science professors at nearby Columbia University before

"There are no rights. The world owes nobody a living."**

Accustomed to dry presentations, Yale students thrilled to the spirit of Sumner's lectures. Life was hard, painful, and difficult, he said. Anyone who said differently was a liar. Governments and organized charities could do little to help the poor and downtrodden. They might even harm them in the attempt.

Sumner certainly used Darwin's theory of natural selection, and the key words *survival of the fittest*, but it would be a travesty to suggest that those were the total of his inspiration. Deeply read, Sumner had come to his conclusions the hard way: through sifting the evidence over many years. His sincerity was never in doubt. When the same student asked whether he would be "sore" if some other professor of political economy came along and took his job, Sumner replied: "Any other professor is welcome to try. If he gets my job, it is my fault. My business is to teach the subject so well that no one can take the job away from me."***

* Richard Hofstadter, *Social Darwinism in American Thought*. New York: George Braziller, 1959, p. 54.
**Ibid.
***Ibid.

bringing *A Civic Biology* to print in 1914. The book did not spend a great deal of time on evolution. Only about seven pages were dedicated to the subject, but in those pages and the diagrams that accompanied them, a high school student could clearly see the thought behind the theory of evolution. As Hunter expressed it:

> Undoubtedly there once lived upon the earth races of men who were much lower in their mental organization than the present inhabitants. If we follow the early history of man upon the earth, we find that at first he may have been little better than one of the lower animals. He was a nomad, wandering from place to place, feeding upon whatever living things he could kill with his hands.[4]

Charles Darwin could hardly have put it better.

For years—a decade in fact—*A Civic Biology* was used in science classrooms around the nation. Tennessee, where the Scopes trial took place, was no exception. During that decade there was very little controversy about evolution in the Tennessee public schools. Perhaps some teachers skipped, or glossed over, the section on evolution. Then again, they may have taught it thoroughly, without upsetting any of their students. All one can say for certain is that there was no cry and uproar until the winter of 1924–1925, when two Tennessee legislators introduced bills, each of which aimed to prevent the teaching of evolution. The bill that won out, gaining the approval of the legislature and the governor's signature, was the Butler Act. It declared:

> It shall be unlawful for any teacher in any of the Universities, Normals and all other public schools of the State which are supported in whole or in part by the public school funds of the State, to teach any theory that denies the story of the Divine Creation of man as taught in the Bible, and to

teach instead that man has descended from a lower order
of animals.[5]

The Butler Act set a fine of not less than $100 and not more
than $500 for each offense. And so, Tennessee became the state,
and Dayton the town, where the teaching of evolution would
be put to the test.

The Forces
Gather

On May 5, 1925, high school science teacher John Thomas Scopes played tennis with some of his students. The game was going nicely, on a slow clay court, when a passerby asked Scopes if he would go to Robinson's drugstore. "Doc" Robinson wished to see him.

The day was quite warm—though the real heat of summer was six weeks away—and Scopes walked the three-quarters of a mile to Robinson's, getting a little sweatier all the time. When he passed through the double doors, one of the town's leading citizens brought him an ice-cold soda pop, and Scopes suddenly noticed that it was not just Doc Robinson who was waiting to see him. Several of the town's leading men were there to greet him. Soon, he was seated with them. George Rappelyea, the manager of a nearby coal

Engineer George Rappelyea *(left)* convinced John Scopes *(center)* to be the defendant in what became the Scopes Monkey Trial. Rappelyea supported evolutionary theory and was interested in the idea of challenging the Butler Act. He also recognized that the town could benefit from the publicity of the trial. Also pictured is Rhea County native and defense attorney Dr. John R. Neal *(right)*, who volunteered his services to Scopes.

facility, put an important matter to Scopes: "John, we've been arguing, and I said that nobody could teach biology without teaching evolution."[1]

That was correct, Scopes said. Seeing that these men were earnest, he went to a nearby bookshelf to fish off a copy of

THE ACLU

The American Civil Liberties Union is one of the most powerful and controversial organizations. Formed to prevent the incursion of the federal government on the rights of individuals, it has—over time— become so powerful that some people question whether it is now dangerous to certain rights and liberties.

In 1917, when the United States entered World War I, many restrictions were put on free speech and the freedom of association. Some high schools forbade the teaching of the German language, and the administration of President Woodrow Wilson took extraordinary steps to ensure that Americans acted in accord with the decision to enter the war. Harvard-educated Roger Baldwin formed the National Civil Liberties Bureau to help people not in sympathy with the war, and he paid a stiff price: going to jail for more than a year. When Baldwin came out of prison, World War I was over, but the government had increased, if anything, its assault on those who did not agree with the basics of American democracy. Red flags had been banned in many states, as showing sympathy with Communism or socialism. Baldwin and two friends reorganized the National Civil Liberties Bureau as the American Civil Liberties Union.

The people who founded the ACLU, and those who guided it through its first two decades, were nearly all New Yorkers with advanced degrees and generally liberal beliefs. Between 1920 and 1980, however, the ACLU showed itself willing to defend the

Hunter's *A Civic Biology*, which had been used in Tennessee schools for the past decade.

"You've been teaching 'em this book?" Rappelyea asked.[2]

Sure enough. Scopes explained that he was the physics teacher, not a teacher of biology, but that he had filled in for that teacher

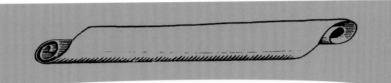

rights of any person—liberal, conservative, or in-between—whose civil rights were threatened by federal, state, or local governments. For example, ACLU lawyers were famed for defending the rights of Nazis, or "skinheads," to march through Jewish neighborhoods (Skokie, Illinois, being a prime example), shouting slogans full of hatred toward Jews. One cannot accuse the ACLU of inconsistency; it defended free speech and the freedom of association wherever those rights were endangered.

By the 1980s, many conservative Americans were convinced that the ACLU only operated on behalf of liberal causes (they were wrong). In the 1988 presidential election between Republican George H.W. Bush and Democrat Michael Dukakis, Bush famously claimed that his opponent was a "card-carrying member of the ACLU."* Up to that time, the ACLU had enjoyed an excellent reputation, but Bush's verbal assault led to questions that have been asked ever since:

Has the ACLU become too powerful?

Do its attorneys only assist those with similar points of view?

The questions will continue, but the ACLU has won its place as part of the fabric of American life. Among similar organizations, only the National Association for the Advancement of Colored Persons (NAACP) is as well known or highly regarded.

---

* "Transcript of the First TV Debate Between Bush and Dukakis." *The New York Times*, September 26, 1988.

when he was ill. Scopes had used this book to review school work with his students for their final exams (the term had ended four days earlier, on the first of May). Scopes turned to page 194 and showed his eager listeners the chart, or diagram, of the evolutionary tree, which featured insects, mollusks, amphibians, reptiles, birds, and—within the section labeled "Mammal"—humankind. As Scopes said, this was the regular textbook, and one could not teach it, or biology, without teaching evolution.

"Then you've been violating the law," Doc Robinson replied.[3]

Scopes was not alarmed to hear this. Like all other teachers in Tennessee, he had heard of the Butler Act, but he, and most of his fellows, thought it would never be enforced. Even the governor of the state had expressed that opinion. At this point, Robinson handed Scopes a copy of the previous day's *Chattanooga News* and called his attention to an advertisement, put there by the ACLU. The advertisement was a call for teachers to step forward, defy the Butler Act, and create a test case in the Tennessee courts. The ACLU pledged to pay the expenses of any defendant and to provide whatever legal counsel was necessary.

Robinson asked if Scopes would be that teacher, the guinea pig.

"I realized that the best time to scotch the snake is when it starts to wiggle," Scopes later wrote in his autobiography, *Center of the Storm*. "The snake already had been wiggling a good long time."[4]

Scopes said yes. If they could prove he had taught evolution and if he qualified as a defendant, he would be willing to stand trial. Minutes later, Robinson went to the only telephone in the drugstore, the type that used a hand crank to generate an electrical charge, and called the city desk of the *Chattanooga News*. He told them that he and his fellows had just arrested a local man for teaching evolution. Undisturbed by the citizen's arrest (he would be formally charged three days later), Scopes went back to his game of tennis.

THE HEAVYWEIGHTS

For the next two weeks, Scopes acted as if his arrest was no big thing, or any kind of controversy. The 24-year-old science teacher later said that he was a naïve fellow at the time. But he was in luck, in that a handful of lawyers came his way, without his having to search for them.

First to arrive was John Randolph Neal, a rather eccentric professor who, after being fired from the University of Tennessee law school, had started one of his own. Just days after Scopes's "arrest," Neal came to Dayton to offer his services, 24 hours a day. Scopes was not sure he needed these services, as the ACLU was supposed to provide counsel. As things turned out, it was fortunate that he had several attorneys from which to choose.

While the ACLU (whose offices were in Manhattan) geared up for the legal contest, millions of Americans were startled by the news that William Jennings Bryan had offered his services, free of charge, to the prosecution. Born in Salem, Illinois, Bryan was one of the most famous Americans of the time. Bryan had been a household name ever since 1896, the year he surprised and stunned the Democratic National Convention with his "Cross of Gold" speech (he argued for a bimetallistic currency, one based on silver and gold, instead of the gold standard alone). Bryan lost the presidential race that year, but he cemented his reputation as the "Peerless Leader" and the "Great Commoner," both of which related to his status with the common, working man. He had run for president two other times, in 1900 and 1908 but had never come close to winning the office. By 1925, Bryan had been on the national stage for about 30 years. Though time had stripped away his once-luxuriant hair and his speaking voice was not as powerful as it had been in 1896, he remained a popular favorite of many Americans, from all walks of life.

Just days after Bryan announced that he would go to Dayton, another heavyweight spoke up.

William Jennings Bryan (1860–1925), right, was known as "the Great Commoner" because he campaigned for farm workers and for the poor. A devout Presbyterian and three-time presidential candidate, Bryan was a long time opponent of Darwinism. Clarence Darrow (1857–1938), left, was one of three lawyers sent by the ACLU to defend Scopes. He had already gained acclaim for his role in the *Leopold-Loeb* case, in which his clients received life in prison instead of the death penalty.

Clarence Darrow was almost universally acknowledged as the greatest defense attorney in the United States. Born in Kinsman, Ohio, he had become a Chicago-based lawyer in his thirties, and, far back in 1896 he had backed his fellow Midwesterner, William Jennings Bryan, for the presidency. The two men had parted ways around 1900, and Darrow had become, first, the most successful attorney defending the rights of labor, and then the most spectacularly successful attorney defending "lost causes." Darrow had enjoyed many remarkable successes over the years, winning millions of admirers and millions of defamers in the process. His most recent "big" case had been that of Leopold and Loeb. In 1924, he had successfully argued against the death penalty for his two clients, young men, who he admitted were guilty of murdering a 14-year-old boy. One would not expect Darrow's position in that case to be popular, but he had argued hard, fast, and well for life imprisonment, as opposed to the death penalty. A lifetime agnostic (someone who takes the view that certain religious claims cannot be proved, and hence, they are unknowable), Darrow believed that the worst thing the state, or courts, could do was sentence a person to death.

NEW YORK

In the beginning of June, John Scopes and John Randolph Neal went to New York City to meet with the leaders of the ACLU. People cautioned Scopes to say as little as possible about the case. He did rather well, most of the time, but he stumbled badly when a newspaper reporter asked him if he was a Christian.

"I'm not sure," he answered. "Who is?"[5]

For many sophisticated New Yorkers, Scopes's answer was perfectly acceptable. To them, the 1920s were a time of widespread skepticism, in which ideas previously held as sacred were now open for debate. But it was otherwise in the American heartland, in states like Tennessee and Ohio, where millions of rural dwellers wanted to turn the clock back to an earlier, simpler time. To them, Scopes's flippant answer underscored the idea that he was a heretic (someone who differs in opinion from an accepted belief or doctrine).

On a lighter note, Scopes was astounded to find that a movie ticket, at certain hours at least, cost $7.50. The *New York Times* and other newspapers delighted in following this rural man around and witnessing his response to aspects of urban life.

Several days into his visit, Scopes was wined and dined by leading members of the ACLU, none of whom wanted Darrow to be part of the defense team. All of them readily acknowledged his brilliance, but, as an agnostic and as a lawyer who had stirred conflicting feelings in any number of trials, they thought he might be too sensational and controversial for the Scopes trial. Scopes remained quiet throughout most of the meal. Then, when asked directly, he said he wanted Darrow. Years later, he explained his decision in his autobiography:

> I was unconvinced that these distinguished barristers were the ones we needed.... It was going to be a down-in-the-mud fight and I felt the situation demanded an Indian fighter rather than someone who had graduated from the proper military academy.[6]

And so it was settled. William Jennings Bryan, the nation's greatest orator, joined the prosecution team as assistant prosecutor, and Clarence Darrow, the country's most successful defense attorney, would be the unofficial head of the defense team. Of course, there were other members of the two teams.

Thomas Stewart, attorney general for eastern Tennessee, would be the chief prosecutor. Besides having Bryan on the team, Stewart would be assisted by Bryan's son, William Jennings Bryan Jr., Wallace Haggard, Sue and Herb Hicks, and Ben McKenzie, an elderly gentleman who had once been attorney general.

Dudley Field Malone, of New York and Paris, would serve as co-counsel for the defense. He and Darrow would be assisted by Arthur Garfield Hays, Frank McElwee (a local attorney), John R. Neal, and William T. Thomas (Darrow's legal associate).

No one wished to call attention to the fact that the case had slipped from the hands of the ACLU, which played only a secondary role in the events that followed.

THE VIPER OF BALTIMORE

Even as the legal teams gathered to size each other up, a flock of newsmen announced that they too would go to Dayton. Television stations like the Columbia Broadcasting System (CBS) were not yet born, so a handful of radio stations as well as a host of newspapermen would carry the weight of the story. Though hundreds of newsmen went to Dayton, one claimed more attention than all the rest combined. This was H.L. Mencken.

The United States has never had a social critic as astute, as biting, and as venomous as Mencken. Born in Baltimore to German immigrants, he grew up an admirer of the German Empire, and during the First World War he was practically muzzled by his newspaper, the Baltimore *Evening Sun* because of his pro-German essays. Soon after the war ended, Mencken was back to front-page headlines, with his devastating attacks on many, if not most, sections of American society. Almost nothing escaped the torment of his pen. Mencken criticized the Wilson administration for entering World War I and for its attack on civil liberties, New Englanders for their smug attitude of cultural superiority, and westerners, especially Californians, for their lack of culture.

Though Mencken went after almost everyone and every-thing, he had a special hostility against the southern states, those that had once made up the Confederacy. One of his most controversial essays—which has been reprinted and discussed countless times since its publication in 1920—was "The Sahara of the Bozart." Mencken lamented the state of learning in the south and attacked the self-importance of its citizens:

> For all its size and all its wealth and all the "progress" it babbles of, it is almost as sterile, artistically, intellectually, culturally, as the Sahara Desert. There are single acres in Europe that house more first-rate men than all the states south of the Potomac; there are probably single square miles

Henry Louis "H.L." Mencken (1880–1956) was one of the most influential journalists of the first half of the twentieth century. He attacked ignorance, intolerance, the middle classes, the elites, fundamentalist Christianity, and people of various ethnic groups. Mencken's columns from Dayton for the Baltimore *Sun* caricatured the local citizens, referring to them as "backwards," "yokels," and "morons." Mencken was the first to use the name "Monkey" trial.

in America. If the whole of the late Confederacy were to be engulfed by a tidal wave tomorrow, the effect upon the civilized minority of men in the world would be [negligible].[7]

Since the Civil War (and one could argue *because* of the Civil War), the southern states had fallen far behind their northern counterparts in learning. By 1920, the south had just about recovered, materially, from the War Between the States. Intellectual and cultural advancement would take a long time. At least Mencken was an equal-opportunity offender; he criticized virtually every part of the country and skewered many of its leading men and women. He did, however, have a special dislike for William Jennings Bryan and the farmer mentality that had governed Bryan's three runs for the presidency. As a newsman, he had first covered Bryan during the Democratic National Convention of 1912, and he had come away far from impressed. Bryan, he wrote, excelled in simplistic thinking and in raising the hate within his listeners.

Mencken disdained, even loathed, the rural mentality that he believed still governed the United States. A rationalist, skeptic, and believer in the advance of progress through science, Mencken felt that Bryan and those who followed him were a danger to the country.

THE ARRIVALS

Bryan arrived first, on July 7, 1925. He got off the train like a hero, to the cheers of the crowd. There were those who noticed that his speech was not as quick as in the past and that he needed his pith helmet (which people usually wore while on African safari) to protect his bald head. To many, however, his arrival in Dayton was the greatest event of the past decade.

Darrow came one day later to much less fanfare. Still, he, too, knew the value of good publicity. Even though he and Scopes knew each other from their New York meeting, the two shook hands for the cameras as if this was the first time they had laid eyes on one another. Darrow looked old, craggy, but formidable.

Mencken was already in town. He was somewhat surprised, he admitted, by Dayton. He had come expecting to find a run-down place with a faint whiff of the Civil War about it. Instead, he found it a place of charm and beauty. Nevertheless, his daily report to the Baltimore *Evening Sun* generally condemned the simple-minded attitudes of the people. To Mencken, they were 100 years behind the times.

Judge and Jury

The American courtroom of 1925 was different enough from the one we know today that most of us would be flummoxed by some of the proceedings. Still, it was similar enough that most modern-day Americans would be able to understand it after some study. The same cannot be said in reverse, because of the many laws passed since 1925 (especially those in favor of the defendant) and because of the many new types of evidence, including the use of lie-detector tests and DNA, which were unknown in the early twentieth century.

THE JUDGE

Dayton did not have a regular court that operated year-round. Instead, it was part of a circuit system in which a judge passed

The second floor of the Rhea County Courthouse in Dayton, where the Scopes Monkey Trial was held, was restored to its original appearance in 1979. The basement houses such memorabilia as the microphone used to broadcast the trial, photographs, and trial records. Every July, local citizens re-enact key moments from the trial.

from one part of his (riding) circuit to another. Judge John T. Raulston had been the judge of the eighteenth district for the previous seven years. A hardworking, simple man, Raulston was a devout Baptist.

Some members of the defense team wanted to shift the trial to Chattanooga or Knoxville, but this was practically impossible. From the very beginning, Dayton supporters like Doc Robinson had seen the event as a heaven-sent opportunity to lift Dayton from obscurity, to put it on the national map. Judge Raulston, too, saw the trial as an opportunity. His desire for the limelight was nearly palpable.

THE ATTORNEYS

Minutes before the trial began, Clarence Darrow and William Jennings Bryan sat for a few moments of conversation. No one was close enough to catch the drift of their words, but the photographs of the time emphasized the differences between them. Both men looked serious, but Darrow's craggy face accentuated what some people thought was his nastiness. Bryan's open expression but closed mouth suggested to many that here was a religious zealot, one without mercy for the sinner.

The lesser-known attorneys had a few minutes to size one another up. Prosecutor Ben McKenzie was the friendliest, most outgoing member on either side, and Dudley Field Malone, who insisted on wearing a double-breasted suit in the heat, was the chilliest, or frostiest, at least on the surface.[1] The defense team was eager to take the measure of Attorney General Tom Stewart, for he was a different kind of southern lawyer; some people called his type the "New South," meaning that he was as up-to-date as any northerner in a similar situation.

THE JURY

The case of *The State of Tennessee v. John Thomas Scopes* commenced on Friday, July 10, 1925. After pleasantries between the attorneys and directions from the judge, the selection of the jury began.

Darrow was famed for his ability to sift through a series of potential jurors, finding the ones who might lean his way. Still he faced an uphill battle here, for almost all the 100 men summoned (only white male freeholders served on juries in Rhea County) could be expected to sympathize with the prosecution, not the defense. The questioning of each juror began with Judge Raulston, proceeded to Ben McKenzie for the prosecution, and then concluded with Clarence Darrow, acting for the defense team.

The first man to be considered was W.F. Roberson, a householder, 30 years old. He rented the farm on which he lived. The key question Darrow put to him was:

"Are you satisfied that you could try it with perfect fairness to both sides?"[2] Upon hearing an affirmative answer, Darrow said the defense would accept him as a juror.

The second man to be questioned was J.W. Dagley, a farmer who lived about 13 miles (21 km) from Dayton. Upon questioning, he revealed that he was a Methodist and that he had children of school age. Darrow asked if Dagley had any personal opinions about evolution. When Dagley replied that he did not, Darrow told him to take a seat, making him a juror.

The third man up was Jim Riley. His thick dark glasses contrasted strongly with his dark blue clothes, making for a strange appearance. The judge found him capable as a potential juror, the state passed him with no questions, and Darrow went to work in his nonchalant way:

Q. Do you know Mr. Scopes?
A. I just know him—I just saw him once—just one time.
Q. Are you a member of any church?
A. Yes, sir.
Q. What one?
A. Baptist.[3]

If there was one thing Darrow knew for certain, it was that he could not avoid having religious men—churchgoers—on the jury. But he continued to probe, asking what kind of prejudice Riley might have. When none was revealed, Darrow asked if Riley had ever read anything by William Jennings Bryan on the subject of evolution.

"No sir, I can't read."[4]

Stumped, for once, Darrow agreed to seat Riley, but minutes later he came back to him, asking:

"You said you couldn't read. Is that due to your eyes?"

"No, I am uneducated."[5]

Darrow showed no sign or response, but others on the defense team were immensely impressed. The answer was so straightforward, so dignified, that they felt here was a man who would try the case in a fair manner. Riley was accepted, and the process moved on to the Reverend J.P. Massingill.

Under questioning, Massingill revealed that he held four pastoral appointments, acting something like a circuit preacher in that part of Tennessee. Darrow pressed, asking if he had ever preached on the subject of evolution, to which Massingill replied that he had never chosen evolution as the topic of a sermon but had referred to it in discussing other subjects. When Darrow went one step further, asking in what way he had preached, Massingill answered, "Well, I preached against it, of course!"[6]

Applause was heard in the courtroom, but Darrow had won his point. He challenged this potential juror for cause. Next up was an elderly man, who asked to be excused on account of his age. The court released him, and the process moved to W.D. Taylor, a farmer who lived 10 miles (16 km) east of Dayton. Darrow's questioning brought out that Taylor was a Southern Methodist and that he had been present at the preliminary hearing of the Scopes Trial. Darrow worked with this for some time, probing as to whether Taylor could be fair and open-minded, but he eventually accepted him, and the selection moved to 43-year-old Tom Jackson.

Jackson was from Spring City, and he had served in the U.S. Army in his twenties. Like almost all the panelists, he was a farmer. Darrow questioned him closely and eventually got to the heart of the matter:

> Q. Have you got a strong opinion one way or the other on evolution?
> A. Yes, I have my opinion on evolution, yes.
> Q. Do you know where you got it?
> A. I got it from the Bible.[7]

Darrow used a peremptory challenge (the right to reject a potential juror without having to give a reason—he was allowed three) to have Jackson dismissed, but as the plain-talking farmer descended from the stand, Darrow said, in a distinctly audible tone, that he believed Jackson was an honorable man. Coming from Darrow, that was high praise.

R.L. Gentry came next. He lived about two miles (three km) from Dayton, and was a teacher during the fall term and a farmer in the spring and summer. Under Darrow's questioning, he revealed that he had read the books on evolution and had taught the subject. Recently, he had read two magazines on the subject: one was *The Conflict*, and the other was *Present Fruit*. The latter claimed that evolution and creation were irreconcilable, that they could not go together. If Darrow was surprised to find so friendly a voice in the courtroom, he did not show it, but passed the man back to the prosecution, which accepted him at once.

J.C. Dunlap came next. He claimed not to have formed a definite idea on the subject of evolution, but under examination from Ben McKenzie, he admitted that he had participated in some loud, even enthusiastic discussions on the subject at F.E. Robinson's drugstore. The court excused him for cause.

Then came W.A. Ault, a merchant who lived in Dayton. A married man and a member of the Baptist church, he had an answer different from nearly all his fellows when asked about evolution:

"You have a definite opinion about it?"

"To a certain extent. I believe evolution is progress, or whatever you want to call it."[8]

The defense excused him for cause, and the court then excused Will Weir. Then came a well-groomed, rather overweight man, who carried a cold cigar in his hand. His name was J.R. Thompson, and he had been a United States marshal during the administration of Woodrow Wilson (Darrow claimed he would not hold this against him). A Methodist, and a freeholder in the county, he was accepted for the jury.

A TOWN OF CRABBES AND KELLYS

"Try to picture a town made up wholly of Dr. Crabbes and Dr. Kellys, and you will have a reasonably accurate image of it [Dayton]."

Crabbes and Kelly sound like characters from a novel, but H.L. Mencken, who wrote this dispatch on Saturday, July 11, had taken them from real life.

Little is known of Dr. Crabbe, other than he was a leader in the Anti-Saloon League, which helped bring about the Nineteenth Amendment, banning the use of alcohol. Mencken, who loved German beer, was naturally opposed to Prohibition. Much more is known of Dr. Howard A. Kelly, the fourth person appointed to the faculty of Johns Hopkins University in Baltimore.

Born in New Jersey in 1858, Kelly graduated from the University of Pennsylvania, then underwent medical training at the same place. He chose the relatively new field of obstetrics and gynecology, and, in 1888, he performed the first successful cesarean section in Philadelphia in more than 50 years. His fame increased as he moved from Philadelphia to Baltimore. By the time he came to know Mencken socially, Kelly had developed the reputation of a saint.

Even Mencken would not deny Kelly's virtues. He was immensely skilled in surgery, a formidable researcher who won appointments and awards by the dozen, and to top it all off, he was the kindest and most helpful of men. Where he and Mencken differed was on the condition of the average man or woman. Mencken believed they needed distractions (including liquor) to escape the tedium of their lives, while Kelly thought they should uplift themselves through sport, exercise, and the use of their mental faculties. In his dispatch to the

(continues)

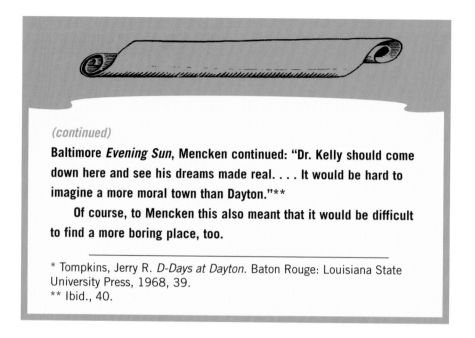

(continued)

Baltimore *Evening Sun*, Mencken continued: "Dr. Kelly should come down here and see his dreams made real. . . . It would be hard to imagine a more moral town than Dayton."**

Of course, to Mencken this also meant that it would be difficult to find a more boring place, too.

***

* Tompkins, Jerry R. *D-Days at Dayton*. Baton Rouge: Louisiana State University Press, 1968, 39.
** Ibid., 40.

Next came W.B. "Squire" Smith, Jess Goodrich, J.H. Bowman, Bill Day, and R.L. West, who were all accepted. After W.P. Ferguson was challenged for cause, the jury of 12 was rounded out by J.S. Wright, a farmer from Spring City. The whole process had taken only two-and-a-half hours. Nineteen men had been examined, and only seven had been challenged or excused.

A photograph, taken of the judge and jury, showed a composite group of Tennesseans. Almost all of them were on the tall and lean side, and nearly all preferred overalls to suits, though they would wear their suits for the trial. The only sour note about the jury came from H.L. Mencken, who, typically, damned the selection and the process as hopelessly backward.

ADJOURNMENT

By now it was three in the afternoon, and everyone was weary. The scientific specialists that the defense had brought to Dayton were especially so. None of them were being paid for their time, which they had volunteered for the cause of science.

Standing at far right is Judge John T. Raulston, next to the jury for the Scopes Monkey Trial. Ralston frequently clashed with Clarence Darrow and was accused of being biased toward the prosecution. The jury included 10 farmers, a schoolteacher, and a clerk.

Seeing the looks on the different faces and knowing that little could be accomplished in the hour that remained, Judge Raulston announced his intention to adjourn for the day. He gave a speech to the 12 men of the jury instructing them not to hold conversations on the topic over the weekend. Raulston was just about to bang his gavel, when Darrow stood up to ask—almost demand—that the men of the jury be sworn in.

Custom was different in Tennessee, the judge replied. The jury would be sworn in after the new indictment was read on Monday morning. Darrow protested, loudly. This was the first time that he had shown much emotion, but it was to no avail. Court was dismissed until Monday morning.

The Heat Sets In

In many places throughout the United States, 1925 was the hottest summer on record. On the very day that the Scopes Trial began, three people died in Manhattan from the heat and about 800,000 New Yorkers went to Coney Island for some refuge from the scorching temperatures. Some records set in 1925 were not broken until 1988, the terribly hot summer that first gave rise to discussions of global warming and climate change.

THE WEEKEND

During the weekend, both teams—the prosecution and the defense—went over their briefs and arguments, rehearsing with each other. Meanwhile, the people of Dayton, and quite a few people with immediate concerns in the trial, did their best to get away from the heat.

John T. Scopes, William Jennings Bryan Jr., and one or two others went to some cold mountain river to dunk their heads. For a few hours Scopes forgot all about the court proceedings. H.L. Mencken did them one better by going to a church meeting on Saturday night. In his aptly titled *Prejudices*, Mencken related what he saw. According to Mencken, there was a preacher of the unordained type. The people attending seemed to be the most ignorant of hillbillies, according to the observer from Baltimore. The most unnerving moments came when a large black woman testified to the presence of the Holy Spirit and began to speak in tongues. Mencken wrote:

> A comic scene? Somehow, no. The poor half-wits were too horribly in earnest. It was like peeping through a knothole at the writhings of people in pain. From the squirming and jabbering mass a young woman gradually detached herself.... Her head jerked back, the veins of her neck swelled and her fists went to her throat as if she were fighting for breath. She bent backward until she was like half of a hoop.... The lady's subjective sensations I leave to infidel pathologists, privy to the works of Ellis, Freud and Moll.[1]

The prose was classic Mencken, biting, scathing, and with the smallest touch of accuracy so that no one could charge him with having invented it.

Court resumed on Monday, the thirteenth of July.

ATTEMPT TO QUASH

Court opened with a lengthy prayer by the Reverend Moffett. The defense then presented a motion to quash the indictment, claiming that it violated the Fourteenth Amendment, which explicitly says that no state may in any way abridge the rights or freedoms of any citizens of the United States. They argued:

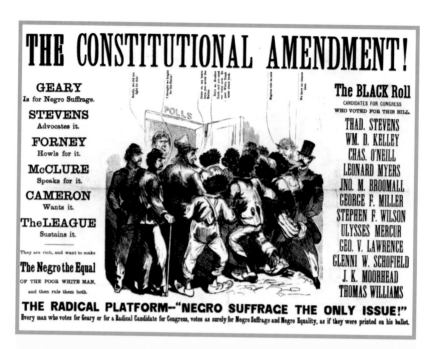

One of the key guarantees of the Fourteenth Amendment to the Constitution is that no one may be deprived of due process of the law. (It also guaranteed full civil rights to blacks after the Civil War ended, depicted in the handbill above). Scopes's attorneys attempted to quash the indictment on grounds that the Butler Act violated Scopes's individual rights and academic freedom, but were unsuccessful.

☆ The Butler Act was unconstitutional in that it embraced more than one subject: the teaching of evolution and the teaching of the biblical story of creation.

☆ The act violated the section of the state constitution that began "Education to be cherished." In part, the section read, "It shall be the duty of the general assembly in all future periods of the government to cherish literature and science."[2]

☆ The act violated the law that required each bill to be read three times before being passed by the legislature.

☆ The act violated the "Right of Worship Free" section of the state constitution.

- ☆ The act violated the section about freedom of the printing presses.
- ☆ The act violated the section concerning the right of each man (they did not use the word *person*) to be undisturbed in his life, liberty, or property.
- ☆ The act and the indictment violated the rights of the accused in criminal prosecutions.
- ☆ The act went against the spirit of the law concerning corporations and individuals.
- ☆ The act violated the law that prohibited one person from holding power in more than one section of the state government.

Just to make triply certain that it presented a strong argument, the defense ended with the words: "The act and the indictment violate Section I of the Fourteenth Amendment of the Constitution of the United States."[3]

John Randolph Neal led for the defense, arguing that Judge John T. Raulston had the right, indeed the duty, to rule on these objections before the trial could proceed. The judge did not wish to see the courtroom empty for a second day in a row, but he needed time, he said, to study the matter. In the meantime, he entertained a motion from Attorney General Tom Stewart for the jury to retire.

Darrow quickly objected, and Stewart answered that there was no issue before the jury at the moment and that it would be prejudicial, or damaging, for the jurors to hear these arguments. Stewart's motion was upheld, and the jury left to go to a back room (by now, they had all been sworn not to discuss the matter).

Neal then went to work:

Our contention, may it please your honor, is that this crime which they have attempted to define—the crime in this act—the definition is so indefinite that it is absolutely impossible for the defense to know exactly the nature of its charge—of the charge.[4]

Neal explained that the statute had two distinct parts, making it illegal to teach evolution and to teach anything other than the biblical story of creation. This, he argued, made it a lopsided and uneven statute, one that could put at risk almost any person teaching in the public schools.

"WE ARE NOT LIVING IN A HEATHEN COUNTRY."*

The dictionary defines *heathen* as "strange" or "uncivilized." Attorney General Tom Stewart's words would not be acceptable in an American courtroom of today or in almost any part of public discourse. This is because twenty-first century America is very different from the America of 1925.

In 1925, the overwhelming majority of Americans identified themselves as Christians. Jews formed a small, but significant, minority that often faced serious discrimination. For example, there were quotas at some Ivy League colleges to prevent too many Jews from gaining admittance. In 1925, a significant, though not overwhelming, majority of Americans identified themselves as of Northern European descent, meaning from the British Isles and the Scandinavian nations. There was a strong bias in favor of Anglo-Saxon customs and Christianity, and those that were "other" tended to be seen as "strange" or "uncivilized."

The census of 1920 revealed that, for the first time in its history, the United States had more people living in urban places than rural ones. That trend would only continue, with the major cities of New York, Chicago, Detroit, and Los Angeles gaining in

Defense attorney Arthur Garfield Hays then spoke, to elaborate on Neal's argument and to go further, into the matter of jeopardy. The Butler Act was only possible under the police powers of the state (the ability of the state to enforce certain behaviors), he said, and those powers were in question here.

Ben McKenzie rose for the prosecution to argue just the opposite. He agreed that there were, at times, laws that were too complex and had too many sections to them. But it was not

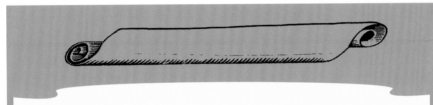

population every year. Coincidental to that was a growth in the idea of pluralism—that all Americans were equal and should be treated as such.

The ACLU and the NAACP played major roles in bringing about this shift of opinion. The ACLU made its first major attempt in the Scopes Trial, and the NAACP had to wait until the 1940s before making serious challenges in court.

If any two decades can be seen as decisive, they would be the 1920s and the 1960s. In the 1920s, a large majority of Americans believed that the nation would continue to echo Anglo-Saxon, Protestant, and Northern European themes for centuries to come. During the 1960s, Jews, Muslims, feminists, and other groups (sometimes called "splinter groups") made significant headway in their quest for equality. By 2009, the year that the first African American was inaugurated as president, it was almost inconceivable for someone to use the word *heathen* in public discussion.

The World's Most Famous Trial: Tennessee Evolution Case, Cincinnati: National Book Company, 1925, p. 66.

the case here, he argued. Any 16-year-old boy could understand the Butler Act after reading it once or twice. McKenzie raised the ire of the defense when he maintained that there were so many out-of-state lawyers in the courtroom (on one occasion he labeled them "foreign"), men who had not been trained under the Tennessee bar. That brought Dudley Field Malone to his feet. He resented the use of the word *foreign*, pointing out that all non-Tennessee members of the defense were citizens of the United States.

Judge Raulston tried to put Malone at ease. "Colonel Malone, you do not know General McKenzie as well as the court does. Everything he says is in a good humor."[5]

Perhaps it was kept off the official court record, for accounts differ, but it seems that the prosecution and defense teams were truly angry with each other that morning. Some reports have Ben McKenzie saying "I love you" toward the defense, with Clarence Darrow snarling in reply, "Sure you do."[6]

Attorney General Tom Stewart rose to make a lengthy rebuttal to the defense's argument. He argued that the Butler Act was plain on its face—there was no need to try to pick it apart—and that it was the legitimate creation of the Tennessee legislature. The section entitled "Cherish literature and science" he brushed aside as merely advisory. There was no need for the legislature or the courts to take it as a law. The most important point Stewart made concerned the police powers of the state. As taxpayers and the financial backers of the public schools, the people of Tennessee had the right, acting through their representatives, to establish whatever kind of school system they desired.

Neal rose to argue that the Butler Act gave preferential treatment to the teaching of the Bible. This led to a heated, but also humorous, spate of words between the defense and the prosecution:

Mr. Neal: Does it not prefer the Bible to the Koran?
General Stewart: It does not mention the Koran.

Mr. Malone: Does it not prefer the Bible to the Koran?

General Stewart: We are not living in a heathen country.[7]

THE AFTERNOON

All this time, the heat was rising. The past week had been hot, but the week of July 13–20 was even hotter. At one point, Ben McKenzie fainted. He came to quickly, but it was evident that his was only the most extreme of many cases. There were plenty of windows in the second-floor courtroom, but so many observers stood by them that no air could come in.

Darrow rose to speak, but before he could commence, Judge Raulston heard and declined a motion from Attorney General Stewart to dismiss the jury for the day. Its 12 members were not paying attention. They had heard nothing of the previous arguments, and it was likely that they would hear nothing more that afternoon.

As he began to speak, Darrow thanked Judge Raulston for having given him the honorary title of colonel, which he hoped would stick to him when he returned to Chicago. The judge came right back and said that he hoped for the same.

This was Darrow's style. Though the cagiest of lawyers, and among the shrewdest of men, he affected a down-home country style that was not entirely a cover. He had, indeed, been born in rural Ohio and was more comfortable with the machinery and clothing styles of the nineteenth century than the twentieth. Perhaps that was why he always wore suspenders in court, though his opponents claimed he did it for appearance.

Darrow usually started off slowly and then built his case while his voice escalated. As he began to speak about the unconstitutionality of the Butler Act, Darrow fired a cannon shot at William Jennings Bryan, saying that a man who "comes from Florida" was responsible for this "foolish, mischievous, and wicked act."[8] Bryan said nothing.

Darrow went on to outline the philosophy behind the trial. On the one hand, there were those who said that the

The trial took place during the heat of summer. More than 900 spectators packed the courtroom daily. Some reports say up to 5,000 visitors came to Dayton at the height of trial. Due to cracks in the first-floor ceiling and the heat, the trial was eventually moved outdoors beneath the trees.

public could determine whatever was taught in the public schools ("Within reason, they no doubt have, no doubt."[9]). But what if the state were to outlaw the teaching of arithmetic? Would anyone stand by and watch that happen? Should they? He continued:

> Now let us pass up the word "divine!" No legislature is strong enough in any state of the union to characterize and pick any book as being divine. Let us take it as it is. What is the Bible? . . . It is a book primarily of religion and morals. It is not a book of science. Never was and was never meant to be.[10]

Darrow had really warmed to the task by now, and the courtroom was utterly still. Partly, that was due to the extreme heat, but it was also because people paid such attention to Darrow's words:

> How many creeds and cults are there this whole world over? No man could enumerate them. . . . Has the Mohammedan any right to stay here and cherish his creed? Has the Buddhist a right to live here and cherish his creed? Can the Chinaman who comes here to wash our clothes, can he bring his joss and worship it? Is there any man that holds a religious creed, no matter where he came from, or how old it is or how false it is, is there any man that can be prohibited by any act of the legislature of Tennessee?[11]

Like a good lawyer, Darrow proceeded to answer the question he had posed. Yes, it would be entirely possible for the nation to exclude others, and to prohibit others from practicing their faiths, if Thomas Jefferson (a big hero throughout the nation, but especially in the south) had not woven his statute of religious freedom into the Virginia State Constitution, and from there into the Bill of Rights:

> [It] has stayed there like the flaming sword to protect the rights of man against ignorance and bigotry, and when it is permitted to overwhelm them, then we are taken in a sea of blood and ruin that all the miseries and tortures and carrion of the Middle Ages would be as nothing.[12]

According to Darrow, the United States had been founded by men who were Christians, and Christians formed a large majority of its population, but it was not formed *as* a Christian nation. To do so would mean to throw out millions, if not tens of millions of people—like the Chinese laborers who had made San Francisco the great city it was.

By now, Darrow had many of his listeners in the palm of his hand. This was an old trick of his, to reason (not always logically) in such a way that he first gained the respect, then the admiration, of his listeners. When he felt himself in control, Darrow became very excited, sometimes snapping the red suspenders over his shirt. He used every kind of gesture known to humans, but he did so in a way that made them listen to his words.

At 4:30, Judge Raulston broke in to say that he was sorry, but the time had come to adjourn. Darrow asked for a few more minutes, five or ten, and the judge told him to continue the next day. Ignoring this, Darrow charged on for another five minutes, building a nearly palpable scene in the minds of his listeners. Those blessed with vivid imaginations could practically feel the heat of the Spanish Inquisition, which had tortured so many heretics, or that of the Roman Inquisition, which had told Galileo to cease and desist with his theory about Earth revolving around the Sun.

Six Thousand or Six Hundred Million

Tuesday, July 14, was the third day of the trial. As he had each day, Judge John T. Raulston asked a local minister to deliver an opening prayer. The defense had been quiet on the matter until now, when Darrow rose to ask that prayer not be used.

This quickly evolved into a spat between the defense and the prosecution, with the latter maintaining that the United States was a God-fearing country and the former saying that opening prayers were prejudicial, in favor of the state prosecution. Raulston overruled Darrow's motion but said he would take the matter under consideration. The judge then spoke to the biggest question at hand: his response to the reasons the defense had brought forward, asking that the indictment be quashed.

He had worked all he could, Raulston said, but everyone knew that Dayton had experienced a big thunderstorm on Monday evening, and his electric lights had been lost for hours. He was not ready, therefore, and would render his decision that afternoon. The court recessed early, with orders to return at 1 P.M.

THE MEDIA

When court resumed, Raulston was not in his typical good humor. He announced, rather angrily, that his decision on the motion to quash the indictment had somehow been leaked to the newspapers, and that, from a telegraph wire, the St. Louis *Post Dispatch* had learned of his choice.

It seemed impossible. How, even in 1925, could the judge's decision be discovered and relayed to St. Louis with such

FUNDAMENTALISM

The word entered the English language in the 1920s, but it came from a series of pamphlets, published between 1910 and 1915. Written by a team of authors, *The Fundamentals* were sponsored by two wealthy men, who made sure that the pamphlets went out to reach about 4 million people throughout the United States.

What the authors of *The Fundamentals*—and their readers—objected to was the growth of Modernism in the Protestant churches. Thanks to developments in science and theology, many Protestant denominations had embraced more liberal ways of thinking, and their ministers were trained in a more open form of preaching. The conflict between Fundamentalism and Modernism dated from about 1890, but it reached a climax in the 1920s.

speed? Questioning of reporters led to the following answer. A newspaper reporter, walking across the lawn with Raulston, had casually enquired when the decision would be given. From Raulston's answer, the reporter had drawn the conclusion that the decision was in the negative, and he had quickly wired the St. Louis newspaper.

Once he found out how the "leak" occurred, Raulston relaxed a bit, but he lectured all the members of the media present. There was to be no repetition of this sort of behavior or he would hold them in contempt of court. He then proceeded to another matter: the question of prayer.

The defense presented a petition, signed by a rabbi, two Unitarian ministers, and one Congregational minister, asking that the judge consider using ministers other than the Fundamentalist ones who had already led the prayers. Raulston

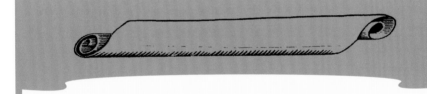

Fundamentalists believed (and still do) that the Word of God, in the Old and New Testaments, was to be taken literally. If the Bible said it had taken 40 years to cross the Sinai Desert (after the departure from slavery in Egypt), then it was so.

Modernists believed (and still do) that the Word of God, whether in the Old Testament or the New, was written for a particular people in a particular time period, one in which belief in miracles was much greater than it is today. While accepting the spirit of the words of the Old and New Testaments, Modernists believed that the literal word was not always accurate.

The Scopes Trial was, perhaps, the single greatest clash between Fundamentalism and Modernism, but it was by no means the last.

The town of Dayton was a strict, religious community. Despite Darrow's objections, Judge Ralston asked a religious leader to pray at the beginning of each court session. Bryan called the trial "a contest between evolution and Christianity . . . a duel to the death."

handled this deftly, saying that names of ministers from all around the county would be placed in a hat, and one name would be drawn each day to see who would offer the morning's prayer.

And that was all for the third day.

WEDNESDAY, JULY 15

In the morning session on July 15, Raulston handled the motion to quash the indictment. His response, which ran to 20 typed pages, was as follows:

☆ It was not necessary for the statute to list everything that could come up in a legal situation.

☆ The court had no jurisdiction to handle the question of whether literature and science were cherished under the Butler Act.

☆ Teachers' rights were not violated under the Butler Act.

☆ There was no special culpability or jeopardy under the Butler Act (everything in the act was clear and obvious).

The most difficult section of the motion was its application to the Fourteenth Amendment, and Raulston ruled on this. He cited a case in Nebraska law, which had upheld the right of that state to prohibit teaching in any language other than English. Raulston concluded: "The court, having passed on each ground chronologically, and given the reasons therefore, is now pleased to overrule the whole motion, and require the defendant to plead further."[1]

The case would continue.

WITNESSES

That afternoon, the state called its witnesses. Eight were called, but only five were found available. The jury was brought back into the courtroom. So far, it had been excluded from hearing almost all that had transpired.

The foreman of the jury, J.R. Thompson, asked that electric fans be provided. So far, there was only one in the courtroom, and it was keeping only the judge relatively cool. Ben McKenzie said that the county would be pleased to do so, but its treasury was so low that it could not afford to (no one blamed McKenzie, who had himself fainted once already). Dudley Field Malone offered to buy some fans, whereupon Judge Raulston offered to "divide" the use of his fan.

Finally, after three days into the trial, a plea was demanded. John Randolph Neal stood to say that John T. Scopes pled "not guilty" to the charge. Attorney General Stewart then defined the state's theory of the case. Scopes had broken the law and was subject to punishment under the Butler Act, and that was all. Dudley Field Malone rose to offer the defense's theory of the case. According to Malone, the prosecution had to prove both that Scopes had taught evolution *and* that he had denied the validity of the biblical story of creation. Neither charge was sufficient unto itself; both had to be proven.

Malone went on to say that, while he and other members of the defense team believed that there was a conflict between the theory of evolution and the theory of creation, they would present scientific testimony—from leading people in the academic community—to show that many such men believed that there was no such conflict. In other words, evolution and creation could co-exist in the minds of intelligent people. Malone continued, saying that science could not be taught without a discussion of evolution. He explained that the evolutionary theory was vital to many modern scientific concepts and had widespread application in agriculture:

> We expect to show you how vital is the theory of evolution to geology. We expect to offer you testimony as to the gradual building of the earth, its age, and how its age is determined. We expect to show you how by the evolution of the earth's crust it is possible to tell where earthquakes are most likely to occur, so that mankind, for its safety, may have warning.[2]

The question was: Would those experts be allowed to testify?

Malone began by asking to read some of the expert testimony allowed. The prosecution quickly objected, and Judge Raulston said he would defer a decision on the matter until the time came. Therefore, the prosecution began its examination of the witnesses.

Walter White, superintendent of Rhea County schools, came first. He testified that Scopes had been at Central High School in Dayton for a year and that his first conversation with Scopes on the subject of evolution had been on May 4, after the end of the school year. The prosecution then produced a copy of the King James Bible, asking to introduce it into evidence. Defense attorney Arthur Garfield Hays objected, arguing that the King James version was only one of several versions of the Bible. Raulston overruled Hays's objection.

Attorney General Tom Stewart then questioned White. He presented a copy of Hunter's *A Civic Biology* and asked the superintendent to turn to a handful of marked pages. The question was: Had Scopes taught this section? White replied, "It is my understanding that he reviewed the important parts of the book and that he reviewed that part that refers to Charles Darwin's theory of evolution."[3]

Under testimony, it was revealed that Hunter's *A Civic Biology* had been the prescribed biology textbook in Tennessee for several years but that the contract had lapsed in 1924. The state had not made a decision about textbooks for the future, and, in the interim, Robinson's drugstore had continued to sell this book to the Central High School students. Then a handful of high school students came to the witness stand, one by one.

Fourteen-year-old Howard Morgan was the son of a bank officer. He testified that he had studied under Scopes. Attorney General Stewart led him in the direction the prosecution wished to go:

> Yes sir; of this year. He said that the earth was once a hot molten mass, too hot for plant or animal life to exist upon it; in the sea the earth cooled off; there was a little germ of one cell organism formed, and this organism kept evolving until it had got to be a pretty good-sized animal, and then came on land to be a land animal, and it kept on evolving, and from this was man.[4]

Young Morgan continued to testify, revealing that Scopes had classified man as among the mammals. Then it was time for Clarence Darrow to cross-examine Morgan. Darrow walked

Morgan through his earlier testimony, having him repeat much that he had learned in high school biology (the boy appeared to have a good memory). Darrow led him, through questions, to the crucial point of, had mankind evolved from earlier, more primitive forms? When Morgan answered yes, Darrow replied:

> "It has not hurt you any, has it?"
> "No sir."
> "That's all."[5]

There was laughter in the courtroom. Darrow had made the prosecution look silly, for there was nothing different about young Howard Morgan from any other 14-year-old who had been "spared" the trouble of hearing about evolution. Next came Henry Shelton.

Shelton remembered the diagrams from pages 194 and 195 in the text. Since so much of his testimony would only echo that of Howard Morgan, he got off rather easily. When it was Darrow's turn to cross-examine, he followed much the same pattern as before:

> Q. Are you a church member?
> A. Yes, sir.
> Q. Do you still belong?
> A. Yes, sir.
> Q. You didn't leave church when he told you that all forms of life began with a single cell?
> A. No, sir.
>   That is all.[6]

An examination of F.E. Robinson followed, with only one relevant fact emerging, that he sold Hunter's *A Civic Biology* and that he had never heard anything bad come from it. Following his testimony, the state rested its case.

EXPERT WITNESS

As its first witness, the defense summoned Maynard M. Metcalf, a zoologist who lived in Baltimore. At 57, he had been
involved in the study of animals for 40 years. He had lived and
worked in Germany for a time and now held a special research
fellowship (financial support awarded to help further the
careers of academics) from Johns Hopkins University. Darrow
took a long time to present Metcalf's credentials, making sure
that the jury heard of the awards he had won in the pursuit of
scientific knowledge. Finally, Darrow went to the heart of the
matter:

> Q. Are you an evolutionist?
> A. Do you know any scientific man in the world that is not an
>   evolutionist?[7]

Attorney General Tom Stewart was on his feet, objecting to
the question, and his motion was sustained. Darrow took his
witness down another track, asking if evolution could be just
an educated guess. Metcalf answered with crisp certainty:

> The fact of evolution is a thing that is perfectly and abso-
> lutely clear. There are dozens of theories of evolution, some
> of which are almost wholly absurd, some of which are
> surely largely mistaken, some of which are perhaps almost
> wholly true, but ... [w]e are in possession of scientific
> knowledge to answer directly and fully the question: "Has
> evolution occurred?"[8]

From his scientific point of view, the answer was the affirmative.

Darrow continued to lead Professor Metcalf, asking about
different geological eras and the approximate age of Earth.
When he spoke of the Cambrian period, Darrow asked him

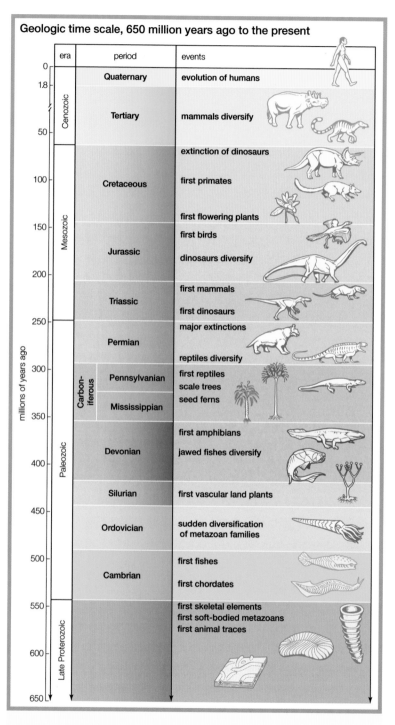

Geologic time scale, 650 million years ago to the present

Pictured is a geologic time scale showing major evolutionary events from 650 million years ago to the present. The approximate age of Earth was contested during the trial.

how long ago that was. Metcalf had no simple answer, so Darrow inquired whether it was more than 6,000 years ago (the age of Earth, according to the calculations of a seventeenth-century bishop). Metcalf answered that 600 *million* years in the past was a reasonable estimate.

A few people in the audience gasped. Others expressed conflicted feelings when Metcalf said that humans were not a particularly advanced species: "Man is not a very highly evolved animal in his body. He isn't as highly specialized as a great many organisms. His hand, for example, is a very generalized structure, nowhere near as much specialized as the hand of a bird."[9]

Metcalf's testimony was the last item of the day. Many people leaving the courtroom believed that the defense had made a rather good showing.

The Greatest
Speech

Thursday, July 16, was the fifth day of the trial. The heat continued unabated, and some reporters began to fade away. They thought that the fireworks were over, and that it was time to get home to write their final reports.

They could not have been more mistaken.

EXPERT TESTIMONY

At the beginning of the day, Dr. Maynard M. Metcalf gave a few more words and was then released from the witness stand. The issue turned to whether Judge Raulston would allow other experts to testify.

Clarence Darrow and the defense team had brought together eight scientists, drawn from different parts of the nation. All were experts in their fields, and most of them had strong connections to organized religion. The point, Darrow said, was to show that men of great intelligence were not necessarily without religious beliefs. But the prosecution brought up any number of arguments to keep the experts off the stand. William Jennings Bryan Jr. rose to state that the advice of experts was unnecessary, for all that the prosecution had to prove was that evolution had been taught. This, of course, led to a series of debates in the courtroom. On strict legal terms, Bryan Jr. and the prosecution were correct, but the trial had, from its very beginning, been about more than the narrow case of one teacher.

Defense attorney Arthur Garfield Hays rose to argue that far more testimony was required:

> Now, as to evolution, does your honor know what evolution is? Does anybody know? The title of the [Butler] act refers to evolution in the schools, but when that is done, you do not know what evolution is. I suppose, ultimately, the jury, because under your [Tennessee] constitution they are the judges, ultimately, of the law as well as the facts, and they will have to pass on the evidence, and that is a question that has been observed by scientific men for at least two centuries.[1]

Hays went on to argue that there were two "Darwinisms," the popular version and the technical one. Darwin and Darwinism had been household terms for half a century, but the American public had never been educated about the precise writings of Charles Darwin. Hays made a good point. If Darwin had been magically transported into the 1925 courtroom, he might well have asked that his theory be considered in the light in which he wrote it, rather than in the way it had been characterized by so many other people, ever since 1859.

Hays argued that the court had the duty to allow the defense to show what evolution was, so that the jury might decide whether Scopes was guilty or innocent. Almost an hour of wrangling followed, with the argument going back and forth. The morning seemed to be going in favor of the prosecution, which made a good argument for keeping the case a narrow one, while the defense kept trying to broaden the scope.

Judge Raulston had found that the Butler Act was reasonable, that it was within the powers of the Tennessee legislature, and that the taxpayers of the state had the right to decide what was taught in their schools. Therefore, the only matter that remained was whether John T. Scopes had, or had not, violated the law.

Again, there was a great deal of wrangling among the attorneys. At one point, a prosecution lawyer asked a defense lawyer if he believed the biblical story of creation. The defense attorney snapped back that it was none of his learned colleague's business.

Seeing that little could be accomplished, Judge Raulston adjourned the session until 1:30 that afternoon.

BRYAN'S SPEECH

When court resumed, Raulston expressed concern about the state of the building. There were almost 400 people on the second floor, and the building had not been designed for such a crowd, or for conditions such as this hot July:

> I do not know how well it is supported, but sometimes buildings and floors give away when they are unduly burdened, so I suggest to you to be as quiet in the courtroom as you can; have no more emotion than you can avoid; especially have no applause, because it isn't proper in the courtroom.[2]

The court was then pleased to have William Jennings Bryan speak.

The Great Commoner had been almost entirely silent, thus far. He had sat, hour after hour, swatting flies and airing himself by use of a large fan he had purchased from F.E. Robinson's

Bryan was known for his deep, commanding voice. At that time, he was thought of as one of the nation's greatest orators. Spectators jammed the courtroom in order to hear the Great Commoner speak.

drugstore. Some in the crowd had been disappointed, but now their moment, and their champion, had come. Thirty years had passed since Bryan's famous "Cross of Gold" speech to the Democratic National Convention, but his voice still held magic, especially for those who looked back at images of a calmer, more peaceful nineteenth century. He began:

> I have been tempted to speak at former times, but I have been able to withstand the temptation. I have been drawn into the case by, I think, nearly all the lawyers on the other side. The principal attorney has often suggested that I am the arch-conspirator and that I am responsible for the presence of this case.[3]

In other words, it was their fault that he was now compelled to speak.

Unlike Clarence Darrow, who began with a folksy introduction and then warmed to his subject, William Jennings Bryan started strong and began to soar. His voice was not as compelling as it had been in 1896, and his appearance had changed as well, but there were many in the courtroom who thrilled to hear the great hero speak once more. In 1893, the country faced a severe economic depression. People blamed the Democrats, the party that held the White House. In 1896, as the Democratic and Populist presidential nominee, Bryan argued at the Democratic National Convention against the use of the gold standard at the expense of the average worker (in a monetary system that uses paper notes, money is converted into pre-set, fixed quantities of gold). He argued for the coinage of silver, too, whose value was set by supply and demand or market rates, not predetermined ratios. The Republicans called for strict observance of gold only. The Democrats, silver miners, and farmers favored free silver. Bryan's limited message resulted in a loss to Republican William McKinley. Now, in 1925, he spoke of the evils of a society that cast off its belief in God: "No, not the Bible, you see in this state they cannot teach the Bible. They can only teach things that declare it to be a lie, according to the learned counsel."[4]

Bryan then used the example of 14-year-old Howard Morgan, who had testified two days earlier:

> I didn't realize it until I saw how a 14-year-old boy understood the subject so much better than a distinguished lawyer who attempted to quiz him. The little boy understood what he was talking about and to my surprise, the attorneys didn't seem to catch the significance of the theory of evolution.[5]

Here, Bryan was on more dangerous ground. He had not studied evolution very deeply. His great talent was to make complicated matters into simple ones, and this time that might not be possible, even with a sympathetic audience. But he had a master card to play. After claiming that evolutionists were insistent on saying that man came from lowly, obscure origins while the Bible asserted they had been created in the image of God, Bryan opened a copy of Hunter's *A Civic Biology*. He opened the book to the diagram on page 194, and asked if Judge Raulston had seen this particular section. Raulston answered that he had not. Well, the court had to see it to believe it, Bryan said.

Page 194 showed that there were 518,000 animal species in the world and that virtually all of them came from the early protozoa. Bryan listed the descent:

> 8,000 protozoa, 3,500 sponges. . . . 360,000 insects. . . . 13,000 fishes. . . . And then we have the reptiles, 3,500; and then we have 13,000 birds. . . . And then we have mammals, 3,500, and there is a little circle and man is in the circle, find him, find man.[6]

There! Humans were not even listed as a separate category; they were simply lumped together in the group of 3,500 species of mammals!

Bryan had the courtroom in his command. He had been in this position many times over the years, and he felt victory in his grasp. Each comment now elicited sparkles of laughter from the crowd. Of course Bryan was right. How could the state of Tennessee allow its youngsters to be taught by a book that did not even recognize human beings by their proper (species) name!

Dudley Field Malone rose for the defense and nearly got into a verbal tangle with Bryan over the subject of Charles Darwin's second book, *The Descent of Man*. Malone noted that it had not been introduced into evidence, whereupon Bryan offered to do so. Malone backed off. He, and the rest of the defense team, knew it would be legal suicide to allow the word *monkey* to take over the courtroom. Had Darwin proposed that humans were related to, or descended from, bears, foxes, or even lions, that might have been acceptable, but there was something about being related to a monkey, an ape, or a chimpanzee that prompted ridicule and derision.

Bryan continued, pointing out that Darwin did not even allow humans to be descended from American monkeys, but rather from *African* ones. Evolution was, quite simply, not in agreement with the dignity of humankind. It preached that humans came from a very low order, when, in fact, they were created in the image of God.

Bryan had one more gauntlet to throw. He brought up Clarence Darrow's cross-examination of 14-year-old Howard Morgan. True enough, the boy had claimed he had not been harmed by the teaching of evolution, but had they asked the boy's mother? Surely, she was more qualified to answer. Here, Bryan invoked the wisdom of the elder generation. He knew his audience. Many in the courtroom, and throughout the American heartland, were disturbed by the skepticism that seemed so abundant in the 1920s.

Though Bryan went on for another 15 minutes, his work was really done. The champion of the people, the Great Commoner, had spoken in defense of the rights of the people of Tennessee to determine what was taught in their schools. They paid the taxes; they had an obvious right to choose.

The defense felt the moment slipping away. They were on the edge of defeat. Rather than send up Darrow (who would be ridiculed as an agnostic), they put up Malone, who had once worked under Bryan, as undersecretary of state in the administration of Woodrow Wilson.

The heat was as difficult this day as on any preceding one. To this point, only two or three men in the courtroom had continued to wear suit coats: One of them was Malone. As he rose to deliver his rebuttal to Bryan, Malone carefully removed and folded his coat. Later, Scopes claimed it was the single most effective gesture of the entire trial.

DUDLEY FIELD MALONE

If the life of William Jennings Bryan exemplified the homespun virtues of rural America, then Dudley Field Malone's life seemed more like a poster for the complexities of the modern, urban world.

Born in New York City in 1882, Malone grew up on Manhattan's West Side. He earned his bachelor's degree at Xavier College and his law degree from Fordham University. His first wife was the daughter of a United States senator.

Malone entered politics around 1910. He was an enemy to the machine politics of Tammany Hall, an organization that had long dominated New York City government. Seen as a reformer, Malone won the attention of President Woodrow Wilson, who made him third assistant secretary of state, under Bryan, who was secretary of state. The two men had conflicted about something (it has never been made clear), and Malone was shifted to collector for the Port of New York. This might have been a comfortable, and quiet, position, had the First World War not intervened. The port was the main staging area for the war effort once the United States entered World War I, and his name was frequently in the newspapers. In 1917, Malone resigned his job as a protest against the way the police treated suffragettes, who were picketing in an attempt to win women the right to vote.

Malone's marriage ended in divorce in 1921. That same year, he went to Paris to marry again (New York laws did not permit him to do so), and over the next few years he became an expatriate, living in the very fashionable Paris of the 1920s. He was much sought after as a divorce attorney.

After the Scopes Trial, Malone continued to live in Paris. He married a third time, this time to an actress. His legal career declined, and in the period just before World War II, he returned to the United States to live in California. His reputation as a fine speaker, combined with his physical appearance, won him parts in several films. He portrayed Winston Churchill in the 1943 movie *Mission to Moscow*.

Malone began with a shot at his one-time State Department chief: "I find it difficult to distinguish between Mr. Bryan, the lawyer in this case; Mr. Bryan, the propagandist outside of this case; and the Mr. Bryan who made a speech against science and for religion just now—Mr. Bryan my old chief and friend."[7]

That was only the beginning. Malone went straight to the heart of the case, claiming that religious leaders and scientists were allowed to differ, that they operated on different grounds, using different methods of evidence: "And what does this law [the Butler Act] do? We have been told here that this was not a religious question. I defy anybody, after Mr. Bryan's speech, to believe that this was not a religious question."[8]

Since Bryan had expanded the boundaries of the case, Malone felt justified in going to any extreme necessary. Before long, he was attacking Bryan and prosecution attorney Ben McKenzie for thinking that they were the only devout people in the courtroom. Surprisingly, Malone won applause on that. He continued:

> These gentlemen say the Bible contains the truth—if the world of science can produce any truth or facts not in the Bible as we understand it, then destroy science, but keep our Bible. And we say "keep your Bible." Keep it as your consolation, keep it as your guide, but keep it where it belongs, in the world of your own conscience.[9]

By now, Malone had the audience as thoroughly in his grip as Bryan previously had. Scientists are often God-fearing men, he said, and they did not try to undermine morality. Instead, their aim was to enlighten the minds of their time. As for children, there was no need to worry about them. The least that this generation—which had emerged from a great and terrible war with 20 million dead—could pass along to the next was all the available data about the world and what was in it. Here,

Dudley Field Malone was one of the lawyers who defended John Scopes. On the fifth day of the trial, Malone delivered one of the greatest speeches of the trial in defense of academic freedom. Even Bryan, one of the nation's greatest orators at the time, told him, "Dudley, that was the greatest speech I ever heard."

Malone scored a point against Bryan's earlier argument as to the wisdom of the elder generation. If the best that people in their forties and fifties could give to young people was the horrors of the Great War, then perhaps younger people were wiser. "Make the distinction between theology and science. Let them have both. Let them both be taught. Let them both live."[10]

Malone went on a bit more, but he had accomplished his great task. In words no less eloquent than Bryan's he had made a strong plea for tolerance.

The applause was so loud that an Irish policeman, who had been "lent" by the city of Chattanooga to Dayton, pounded on a table with his billy club. Hearing this, some of his comrades came upstairs to ask if he needed assistance, to which he answered, "I'm cheering!"[11]

Years later, Scopes remembered the scene. Shortly after Malone's speech, court was adjourned. Almost everyone left, in order to seek relief from the oppressive heat. Soon it dwindled to where only Scopes, Malone, and Bryan were left in the courtroom. Bryan spoke up, telling his one-time subordinate: "Dudley, that was the greatest speech I ever heard!"[12]

Malone replied that he was sorry to have been the person to deliver it.

Out on the Lawn

Judge Raulston called the court to order on the morning of July 17. The heat was as strong as ever, and there were continued fears about the strength, or weakness, of the floor, or even the building's foundation. But court began, just the same.

NO NEED FOR THE EXPERTS

Judge Raulston commenced the session by reading a lengthy ruling. He had studied the matter in depth and decided that the testimony of expert witnesses would not shed further light on the subject. At hand was whether a Tennessee law had been violated and if the people of that state had the right to determine what was taught in the public schools. Whether the theory of evolution was correct was beside the point.

The defense quickly took an exception to the ruling not to use witnesses. A sarcastic exchange followed, with attorney Arthur Garfield Hays suggesting that the court was not acting fairly, Attorney General Tom Stewart acting as if the trial were over, and Clarence Darrow snarling: "Don't worry about us. The state of Tennessee don't rule the world yet."[1]

Hays continued, asking that the court at least allow the expert witnesses to submit written statements, which could be viewed by an appellate court (the court that hears the appeals of a trial court) at a later date. By now, most members of the defense were thinking in terms of the court of appeals. But almost as soon as Judge Raulston agreed to this, William Jennings Bryan was on his feet, asking that the prosecution be allowed to cross-examine the witnesses. That request had Clarence Darrow on his feet, and he and Bryan soon exchanged volleys across the courtroom, with Judge Raulston getting some of the heat of the exchange:

> The Court: Well, isn't it an effort to ascertain the truth?
> Mr. Darrow: No, it is an effort to show prejudice. Nothing else. Has there been any effort to ascertain the truth in this case? Why not bring the jury and let us prove it?"[2]

That was as far as Judge Raulston would permit Darrow to go, but a minute later they returned to their cross-fire:

> Mr. Darrow: We except to it and take an exception.
> The Court: Yes, sir; always expect this court to rule correctly.
> Mr. Darrow: No, sir, we do not. . . .
> The Court: I hope you do not mean to reflect upon the court.
> Mr. Darrow: Well, your honor has the right to hope.[3]

The bare words of the testimony do not reflect the heat of the moment, nor the sarcasm with which Darrow delivered those last eight words. As he did whenever he wanted to get a point across, Darrow hunched his shoulders, pinched his suspenders, and glowered. But he had gone too far.

Raulston did not reply on the spot, saying only that he had the power to do something else, perhaps. Everyone understood that he meant Darrow had placed himself in jeopardy.

Darrow made no apology, and he was quiet for the next half hour while Raulston and Hays worked out the details. The expert witnesses would be allowed to submit affidavits, some of which could be read aloud in the courtroom. The prosecution would have the right to cross-examine anyone who took the stand. This was set for Monday, and at 10:30, Raulston adjourned.

ALL OVER BUT THE SHOUTING

Over the weekend, most of the newsmen packed and went home. The trial had been something of a disappointment, most of them said. There had been some good fireworks in the speeches of Bryan and Malone, but nothing like the thunder and lightning they had hoped for. H.L. Mencken left Dayton over the weekend, too, claiming that all that remained was the "formal bumping off of the defendant."[4] As to shedding light on the theory of evolution, and what could or could not be taught in the schools, the matter seemed as murky as ever.

The prosecution knew that the case was well in hand, and its leading members pursued other interests over the weekend. William Jennings Bryan spoke to a large crowd in Dayton, promising that he would take this fight to other courts in other states and that the forces behind the wisdom of the Bible would prevail.

The defense was far gloomier, but Clarence Darrow held out some measure of hope. Without revealing his exact plan, he told friends that he would place a Bible expert on the witness stand and do to him what he had not been allowed to do with the expert scientific witnesses. Only a few people knew

Dayton became a media circus as it was overrun by reporters, religious fundamentalists, and curious observers. Many journalists and cartoonists ridiculed the trial, characterizing the fundamentalists as backward. In this cartoon, the left side, labeled "Five Months Ago," shows a scruffy mountain man named "Dayton" asleep against the trunk of a mighty oak. The right side, labeled "Today," shows the same man as a giant, all spruced up in a new suit and hat, speaking into an enormous microphone, thinking "This is the life!" He is surrounded by photographers and reporters and the mighty oak has been reduced to a tiny tree.

what Darrow meant, but there were intense practices held on Saturday night. As Darrow had claimed, the state of Tennessee did not rule the world, yet.

THE SEVENTH DAY

The trial resumed on Monday, July 20, 1925. Judge Raulston opened by having the jury retire once more. There were things its members should not hear. He explained to the courtroom that he had not acted on Friday morning, because a judge should never act in the heat of the moment. But he had been deeply offended by Darrow's words, "Well your honor has the right to hope."

Raulston believed he had made every effort to be fair to the attorneys from outside the state, that he had bent over backward at times. But this brazen disrespect could not be passed over. Raulston cited Darrow for contempt of court, requiring him to appear in court the very next day to answer the charge. Bond was set at $5,000. Darrow, naturally, claimed he did not have the money handy, but friends of his immediately volunteered to put it up: There would be no trouble on that score.

Darrow remained quiet, and the trial resumed.

Arthur Garfield Hays offered a new textbook and asked that it be placed into evidence. The readings he selected showed that the author had a high regard for Charles Darwin and the theory of evolution. Then came one expert witness.

The witness was not heard in court, but Hays read aloud a long statement favoring evolution and offering the witness's claim that, in his mind, evolution and the Bible were not mutually exclusive. The court adjourned until 1:30.

When everyone returned to the courtroom, Darrow stood to apologize to Raulston. The apology was as contorted as could be, with Darrow saying he believed he had done nothing wrong, but since the judge did, then the apologies were offered. Darrow made a point of praising the people of Dayton:

I have been treated better, kindlier, and more hospitably than I fancied would have been the case in the North, and that is due largely to the ideas that Southern people have and they are, perhaps, more hospitable than we are up North.[5]

Darrow went on for some time, sounding contrite at one moment and mildly confrontational at the next. But at the end of his apology, he, and almost everyone else, was stunned when Raulston stood, recited some poetry, and publicly forgave Darrow. This was a scene that would not have taken place in a courtroom anywhere else except in the South.

BRYAN AND DARROW

They had known each other for just about 30 years. They represented different visions, and versions, of the American dream.

Both hailed from the rural heartland. Bryan was from Salem, Illinois, and Darrow was from Kinsman, Ohio. Born in 1857, Darrow was three years older, but he looked more than his 68 years. Bryan, on the other hand, had shown signs of heat exhaustion throughout the trial, but his facial expression made him seem younger than 65.

Both men had been raised on heartland values, but Darrow's father had been the village skeptic, raising his son to question much of what he heard, while Bryan's had been the more accepting of the two. They also differed in that Darrow had become a big-city person, living and working in Chicago, while Bryan preferred rural retreats.

They first met in 1896, the year Bryan gave his "Cross of Gold" speech to the Democratic National Convention. Darrow had exchanged letters with a friend the next day, in which both men marveled at Bryan, but in which both posed the question: Just what

Raulston pulled a second surprise. For almost a week, he had worried about the state of the building, and he now declared that, in the interest of the public safety (some people had fainted), he would take the court outside, to the lawn in front of the courthouse.

Though they were surprised, people were also pleased. The heat in the second-floor courtroom was simply unbearable, while the lawn afforded some shade and just the barest hint of a breeze. There also were lemonade stands close by. Everyone packed their things, and about a half hour later the case of *Tennessee v. Scopes* resumed on the bandstand, at the eastern edge of the lawn.

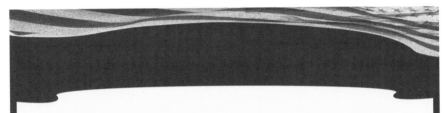

had the man said? Darrow ran for U.S. Congress that year, but he had devoted so much of his time to helping Bryan's election campaign that he lost his own, by the narrow margin of about 100 votes.

Bryan and Darrow had parted ways sometime in the first decade of the twentieth century. By then, Darrow was a confirmed Modernist (some called him an atheist), and Bryan had reverted to the American-heartland view that the Bible was the greatest source of knowledge. Even so, there was no animosity between the two giants until Bryan took up the anti-evolutionary cause in 1922. From then on, Darrow had waited, hoping for just the right moment to expose Bryan's weaknesses. He had submitted questions to a major Chicago newspaper, asking that Bryan answer them, but his opponent had scorned them. Now, on a hot afternoon in July 1925, the men who knew each other well, and who knew the American dream of the nineteenth century that had passed and had some inklings of the dream of the new twentieth century, had one last opportunity to go at each other in a grand style.

Almost everyone seemed relieved. The trial was winding down, the fireworks had been less than expected, and now everyone could catch some decent air. The defense began tamely enough, offering the expert opinion of a legal scholar that the King James Bible was not the only one in existence and that the scholars who compiled it in 1611 may have made some important mistakes in translation. No one, including the prosecution, seemed bothered by this. They had heard something similar the week before.

Then Darrow rose to make exception to a foot-long sign, on one of the buildings near the lawn, which read "READ YOUR BIBLE." He and the prosecution wrangled for some time before Raulston ordered it removed. Then, while everyone was reasonably relaxed, Darrow pulled his master stroke: He asked that William Jennings Bryan come forward, to act as an expert witness on the Bible.

Prosecution attorneys were on their feet in seconds, waving their hands and asking that this ridiculous idea be scotched. There was no precedent for calling an attorney from the opposite side and demanding that he act as an expert witness!

Bryan waved off the actions of his fellows. He was not afraid, he said, and all he asked was that he have the right, later, to question the defense attorneys. When this was granted, Bryan came forward and was seated at the edge of the bandstand.

Darrow began calmly and slowly: "You have given considerable study to the Bible, haven't you, Mr. Bryan?"[6]

Sure enough, he had studied the Bible, to one extent or another, for the past 50 years.

Darrow questioned whether Bryan had given much thought to making interpretations of the Bible. Bryan at once saw this for the slippery slope, and replied that no, he had written what he would call commentaries, but nothing like interpretations.

Q. You claim that everything in the Bible should be literally interpreted?

A. I believe everything in the Bible should be accepted as it is given there; some of the Bible is given illustratively. For instance: 'Ye are the salt of the earth.' I would not insist that man was actually salt, or that he had flesh of salt, but it is used in the sense of salt as saving God's people.[7]

Fair enough. Darrow continued to press. Bryan was doing well, answering rather absurd questions with rather tongue-in-cheek replies, when he stumbled on the matter of Joshua ordering the Sun to stand still in the Old Testament. "Do you believe Joshua made the sun stand still? . . . Do you believe at that time the entire sun went around the earth?"[8]

This was a trick question in the biggest sense of the word. The Catholic Church had denied the Copernican theory that Earth revolved around the Sun, rather than the other way around. Darrow was attempting to make Bryan look foolish.

Q. Mr. Bryan, have you ever pondered what would have happened to the earth if it had stood still?

A. No.

Q. You have not?

A. No; the God I believe in could have taken care of that, Mr. Darrow. . . .

Q. Don't you know it would have been converted into a molten mass of matter?[9]

Now Darrow had scored. Even though many people in the audience did not believe in evolution, especially the obnoxious idea that humans were related to apes, almost everyone believed in the heliocentric (sun-centered) universe. Most understood that Earth had to move or else it would be fried by the heat from the Sun.

Up to now, Bryan had done well, at least keeping even with Darrow. But from this moment on, the questions came faster and faster. Bryan seemed to have no good response. When the two men tangled over the age of Earth, Darrow asked how the biblical experts had ever arrived at their notion that it was 6,000 years old:

> Q. But what do you think that the Bible, itself, says? Don't you know how it was arrived at?
> A. I never made a calculation.
> Q. A calculation from what?
> A. I could not say.
> Q. From the generations of man?
> A. I would not want to say that.
> Q. What do you think?
> A. I do not think about things I don't think about.
> Q. Do you think about things you do think about?
> A. Well, sometimes.[10]

This was the moment—if not the last possible chance—to get Bryan off the witness stand. Tom Stewart began to object furiously, asking where this line of questioning was going. But each time his fellow attorneys protested, Bryan waved them off. He wanted to answer the questions, he said.

Bryan did a little better when Darrow examined him on the subject of ancient cultures and religions. Darrow still worked in points, however. He showed Bryan's ignorance of Asian culture, when Bryan was unable to pinpoint the length of Egyptian civilization, and he continually returned to the question of time. How long had it taken to create Earth? How long had Earth existed?

Bryan tried to rebut, claiming that certain scholars agreed with his view on the age of Earth, but it was revealed that not one of them held a post at a major college or university. The worst moment, though, came about an hour in:

> Q. Do you think the earth was made in six days?
> A. Not six days of twenty-four hours.[11]

In a surprising move, Darrow *(standing, right)* put Bryan *(seated, facing Darrow)* on the stand as a witness on the seventh day of the trial. Darrow questioned Bryan on miracles and events from the Bible in an effort to show that the Bible stories could not be scientific and should not be used in teaching science. Bryan went on the stand with the understanding that Darrow also would have to submit to questions by Bryan.

Some audience members gasped. This was Bryan's most forthright admission that he thought the Bible was not literally true and that one could not trust it as a historical document. Bryan went on to say that the six days might have referred to six "ages" or periods of time, but in so doing he made himself—to his followers—seem little better than all the other scientific witnesses. He was twisting, or perverting, the Bible's truth.

Knowing he had stumbled, Bryan tried to turn the tables. Pointing to Darrow, he nearly shouted that he was not trying to get anything into the record, he was trying to protect the

Bible from the greatest atheist or agnostic in the United States. There was some applause, whereupon Darrow turned to the spectators, frowned, and said he wished he could "get a picture of these clackers."[12]

Stewart objected, each time more furiously than the last, but it was too late. The duel between the heavyweights could not be stopped. Darrow returned to the six days of creation, or the six ages or epochs:

> Q. You think those were not literal days?
> A. I do not think they were twenty-four-hour days.
> Q. What do you think about it?
> A. That is my opinion—I do not know that my opinion is better on that subject than those who think it does.
> Q. You do not think that?
> A. No. But I think it would be just as easy for the kind of God we believe in to make the earth in six days as in six years or in 6,000,000 years or in 600,000,000 years. I do not think it important whether we believe one or the other."[13]

By now, Bryan was almost a wreck on the stand. Sweating profusely, imploring the audience to stay with him, he seemed like a parody of the man who had eagerly stepped to the witness stand an hour and a half before. Bryan's defenders also had a difficult time that afternoon. He was their hero, defending their great book and set of beliefs, but when he spoke of 6 million years or 600 million, he seemed to speak the language of the Modernists.

There was a last, humorous back-and-forth about the snake that tempted Eve with the apple. Darrow poked fun at the idea, asking Bryan if he knew whether this animal had crawled on its belly, as the Bible said.

> A. I believe that.
> Q. Have you any idea how the snake went before that time?

A. No, sir.

Q. Do you know whether he walked on his tail or not?[14]

Judge Raulston released the court at 4:00 in the afternoon.

THE REACTION

The recollections of the many observers varied, as did their memories, when asked years later. It seems clear, however, that Clarence Darrow was approached, even mobbed, by more people and that he received more congratulations than did William Jennings Bryan. To be sure, there were those who felt that Darrow had gone too far, that he had gotten too much in Bryan's "face." But, on the whole, the observers seemed to feel that this part of the trial had revealed more "truth" than any other.

From Dayton to Hollywood

After the fireworks of Monday, it was almost inevitable that the proceedings would cool off a bit. This was true for the seating arrangements. There was a light rain on Tuesday morning, so the judge, jury, and participants had to go back inside the Dayton county courthouse. There would be no more time on the lawn.

INADMISSIBLE

Judge Raulston began the morning session with a short statement. He had pondered the previous day's events and decided that William Jennings Bryan's lengthy testimony as a Bible expert would be stricken from the record. As Raulston put it, Bryan's testimony could not assist this court, or any appellate court, in deciding whether Scopes had broken the law.

Clarence Darrow rose to say that he agreed that Bryan's testimony might not be relevant to an appellate court decision, but also that he wasn't through. He wanted the direct examination to continue. For his part, Bryan scowled from his chair. He wanted desperately to be allowed to interrogate Darrow, Malone, and Hays, but Attorney General Tom Stewart had firmly told him the night before that this charade could not continue.

When Raulston explained his ruling, and repeated it just so all would understand, Darrow announced that the defense had nothing further to offer the court: "I think to save time we will ask the court to bring in the jury and instruct the jury to find the defendant guilty. We make no objection to that, and it will save a lot of time and I think that should be done."[1]

Even this major admission only won a few sighs of relief. The audience was clearly worn out from the previous day's drama.

Bryan was allowed to make a short speech, in which he said he would have to trust the press to make sure that his statements—given the previous day—were not taken out of context. Raulston then summoned the 12-man jury and instructed them in the law:

> You, gentlemen, are the sole and exclusive judges of the facts and the credibility of the witnesses, and the judges of the law under the direction of this court. . . . Under our constitution and laws the jury can have no prejudice or bias either way, but you should search for and find the truth, and the truth alone.[2]

The jury was then sent out. Nine whole minutes passed before the 12 men returned. Most of that time was spent exiting the crowded courtroom and then re-entering. The actual conference of the jury was a matter of but two or three minutes, held in the second-floor hallway.

Back in the courtroom, the jurors returned a verdict for the state: John T. Scopes was guilty. Raulston asked what fine they had set, whereupon he was told that they were satisfied to leave that matter to him. Raulston levied a $100 fine. Scopes then made his first, and last, words in open court:

> Your honor, I feel that I have been convicted of violating an unjust statute. I will continue in the future, as I have in the past, to oppose this law in any way I can. Any other action would be in violation of my ideal of academic freedom—that is, to teach the truth, as guaranteed in our constitution of personal and religious freedom. I think the fine is unjust.[3]

It was over.

AFTERMATH

As they filed out of the courtroom, Dayton's citizens were pressed by the remaining members of the news media. Had the trial lived up to its billing? Had it resolved the question of men and monkeys?

Quite a few people of Dayton expressed dissatisfaction. The trial had never put the major issues to the test. Instead, it had concentrated on the narrow subject of whether Scopes had taught evolution, which anyone who looked at Hunter's *A Civic Biology* could see that he must have done it.

Others showed indignation at the way Darrow had handled Bryan on the witness stand. How could this atheistic lawyer from Chicago act that way toward the Great Commoner, the person who stood for the rural values of the American heartland? Still others confessed to disappointment at the way everyone was fleeing Dayton as soon as the trial was over; perhaps the town "boosters" had made a mistake.

ONE MORE CIRCUIT

One person who knew very clearly what he wanted was William Jennings Bryan. Smarting from his poor performance on the witness stand, Bryan released a series of questions to the newspapers, daring Clarence Darrow to respond to them. By the end of Tuesday, Bryan was again speaking before a crowd of reporters, but he did so defensively, talking about the academic degrees he held and insisting that Darrow did not have a monopoly on scientific knowledge.

A day later, Bryan left Dayton. He went to Knoxville, Tennessee, to give a major speech in front of thousands of people. The great contest, Bryan claimed, had only begun. He would help the people of any state that wished to outlaw the teaching of evolution. He would carry on the fight as long as it took.

This was very much in character for the Great Commoner. Over the past 30 years, he had given thousands of speeches and participated in many elections. He knew, as well as any man, how to bounce back after a defeat.

Leaving Knoxville, Bryan went to Tom Stewart's hometown of Winchester, where he gave a rousing speech to more than 2,500 people. Then it was back to Dayton, where Bryan planned a major speech the next day. There are those who claim that Bryan was acting out of desperation, but they have not studied his career history. Ever since he gave the "Cross of Gold" speech in 1896, Bryan had been this kind of stump speaker.

Bryan's wife expressed concerns in the automobile ride to Dayton. She had never been keen on the anti-evolutionist case, and now she feared that Bryan would lose control of his followers, who might turn this into a crusade against freedom of speech. Bryan gave her a comforting answer, saying he believed he could control them. Reaching Dayton, Bryan enjoyed a large noon meal, then lay down for a nap. An hour or two later, his wife discovered he was dead.

Bryan had suffered from diabetes for some time, and he may have had high blood pressure as well. No autopsy was performed, and the medical report claimed that he died of apoplexy (stroke).

The people of Dayton were stunned. When the news spread, over the telegraph wires, people around the nation could hardly believe it. The Great Commoner had not performed well on Monday, July 20, but he had seemed hale and hearty throughout the trial. True, he had fanned himself more than other participants in the trial, but his sudden death was shocking.

Bryan's corpse was taken by train to Washington, D.C. Because he had raised a regiment in the Spanish-American War, he was buried at Arlington National Cemetery with full military honors. Before that, however, his body lay in state, and thousands of well-wishers came to see the Great Commoner in his casket.

GLOATING AND GLUTTONY

Two things—equally absurd—have been said about William Jennings Bryan ever since his death. Many people blamed Clarence Darrow for Bryan's death, saying that the grilling on the witness stand on July 20, 1925, was too much for the Great Commoner. Darrow did not dignify these claims with an answer, but one can, today, say that it is ridiculous. Anyone who could not handle the heat of verbal combat (and Bryan does not belong in that category) had no business taking the stand in such an intense case. Moreover, Bryan had experienced plenty of setbacks before, including losing three races for the presidency, and he had always bounced back very nicely.

Many others, including H.L. Mencken, blamed Bryan himself, saying that the Great Commoner's gluttony had led to his demise. This can be laid to rest as firmly as the claim that his time on the stand had killed him.

Bryan did have a formidable, some even called it a gargantuan, appetite. He was known for the size of his meals and the length of his meal times. Gluttony was a real part of his makeup, one that he did not try to deny. But to say he ate himself to death is absurd.

Comments ranged from extreme admiration to cynical pleasure. During his long time on the public stage, Bryan had remained constant to his key themes, which revolved around the American heartland, the plight of the farmer, and the need for society to reflect those values. But he had also, at times, been an opportunist, jumping on the bandwagon for causes that seemed likely to improve his status. For example, the anti-evolution crusade began in 1921, but a decade or so earlier, Bryan had written in favor of tolerance on that issue.

The many photographs from the Scopes Trial show a Bryan who was overweight, perhaps by as many as 30 pounds (14 kilograms), but the same could be said for many of the other attorneys involved (it could not be said of the jury, made of up lean, lanky farmer types).

Along with his roaring appetite, Bryan had undergone a life of exertion, first in farm work in his youth, then as a newspaperman, and finally as a public figure who practically raced from one train station and hotel to the next. He was physically fit in the sense that he was able to keep up with his demanding schedule.

To claim that Darrow "killed" Bryan with his cross-examination is akin to saying that one professional athlete kills another by winning a race or a match. Racehorses do not die of broken hearts, and neither do top-notch politicians. To suggest that Bryan died from overeating is just as ludicrous, and mean-spirited.

This is not to say that one should hold Bryan up as a model of physical fitness. Rather, one can take away the impression that the newspapers of the time did Bryan a cruel injustice, explaining his demise to eating habits, when, in fact, his time had simply come.

On July 26, five days after the end of the trial, Bryan died in his sleep after spending several days and hundreds of miles traveling and speaking to crowds of more than 50,000. Because of his past service during the Spanish-American War, Bryan was buried in Arlington National Cemetery. A steady procession of mourners paid their respects before he was taken to his final resting place.

The greatest denunciation came, as one might expect, from the pen of H.L. Mencken. In his *Prejudices, Fifth Series*, Mencken blasted Bryan:

> Bryan lived too long, and descended too deeply into the mud, to be taken seriously hereafter by fully literate men, even of the kind who write school-books. There was a scattering of sweet words in his funeral notices, but it was no more than a response to conventional sentimentality. The best verdict the most romantic editorial writer could dredge

up, save in the eloquent South, was to the general effect that his imbecilities were excused by his earnestness—that under his clowning, as under that of the juggler of Notre Dame, there was the zeal of a steadfast soul.[4]

Mencken's biting sarcasm turned many of Bryan's followers into even stronger true believers, but for Americans on the fence, the barbs from Baltimore had some effect.

No one else would claim that Bryan had lived too long, but many would agree that he had been on the public stage too long.

THE PARTICIPANTS

John T. Scopes, who had played very little of a role during the trial, was besieged with letters from all over the country. Some offered him roles in movies; others threatened him with bodily harm; while still others contained marriage proposals from eligible young women. Scopes studiously ignored them, and eventually he and a good friend made an enormous bonfire of the letters in a backyard.

By the autumn of 1925, Scopes had embarked on a new life, as a graduate student in geology at the University of Chicago. One of the scientific experts, Dr. Kirtly Mather, had arranged for Scopes to receive a scholarship. Scopes headed off to the big city, and a very different life, but he remained the quiet, unassuming country boy. He never made any money out of the Scopes Trial and never expressed a wish to have it any different. Clarence Darrow remained his big hero throughout life. Scopes said that, next to his father, Darrow had the biggest influence on him.

Darrow continued to practice law. He never had so sensational a case again, but he plugged on. He continued to fight what he considered incursions on academic freedom, the freedom of speech, and the freedom of assembly. His reputation, already great in 1925, rose to such a height that many courtroom lawyers, portrayed on the stage or on television, were to some extent based upon him. Suffering from heart disease, Darrow was unable to practice law in the last decade of his life.

H.L. Mencken "peaked" as a journalist in the 1920s. The stark contrast between urban America—which he claimed to represent—and rural America, for which he affected scorn, was never greater than in that decade. Mencken's popularity and success waned during the 1930s. A staunch individualist, he opposed President Franklin D. Roosevelt's New Deal, which sought to alleviate the poverty of Americans during the Great Depression. Mencken's editorials against Roosevelt and the New Deal caused his popularity to wane. Like Darrow, he spent the last decade of his life out of the public limelight.

Attorney General Tom Stewart had, perhaps, the best second act. Of all the lawyers connected with the Scopes Trial, he was the only one to emerge with his reputation fully intact, having won the good opinion of men on both sides of the bar. Stewart went on to be a U.S. senator from Tennessee, serving in the 1940s.

THE PLAY

The Scopes Trial remained vivid in the minds of most Americans. Even for a decade that saw the advent of radio, the automobile, and the rise (and crash) of the stock market, the Scopes Trial stood out. Perhaps it was because of the intense heat of 1925, which was remembered for decades afterward.

As the thirtieth anniversary of the case approached, two New York City playwrights decided to use the trial as a means of discussing current events. The so-called McCarthy Era (named for Senator Joseph McCarthy of Wisconsin) was a time when ordinary Americans felt under assault for their beliefs. It was a time when small groups of activists denounced people as Communists or socialists, condemning them in the court of public opinion. *Inherit the Wind*, the Broadway play, was the result.

Even though the directors had a prelude, in which they declared that the play was not strictly historical, many people began to "see" the Scopes Monkey Trial through the lens of

In 1955, the play *Inherit the Wind* was produced loosely based on the Scopes Trial. In 1960, *Inherit the Wind* was made into a film starring Spencer Tracy *(left)* and Frederic March *(right)* as characters based on Darrow and Bryan.

Inherit the Wind. This was even more the case when Hollywood saw the opportunity to capitalize on the subject.

Inherit the Wind, the movie, came out in 1960, with Spencer Tracy starring as a lawyer based on Clarence Darrow and Frederic March as a lawyer based on William Jennings Bryan. Gene Kelly played a journalist based on H.L. Mencken. The casting was excellent, with the tart-tongued Spencer Tracy convincing in his role as the seeker of truth and the close-lipped Frederic March acting like Bryan.

The film stuck close to the historical record in many respects, but, to make things more exciting, there was a supposed romance between the person who personified Scopes and the daughter of a prominent minister of the town (which was called Hillsborough). There was also a major change, in that the direct examination of Bryan by Darrow was conducted inside the courtroom, rather than on the lawn.

What the film did not do was justice to the many people—in 1925 and in 1960—who believed that the Bible and evolution could be reconciled. Both the play and the film made it an either-or proposition, with damning words for anyone who disagreed.

Science Marches On

The year 2009 marked the eighty-fourth anniversary of the Scopes Trial, and the two hundredth anniversary of Charles Darwin's birth. Both anniversaries helped to refocus attention on evolution, creationism, and what should be taught in the public schools.

DARWINISM IN 2009

Two hundred years had passed since Darwin's birth and 150 since the publication of *The Origin of Species.* Most scientific generalists continued to hail Darwin as one of the most important minds of human history and *The Origin of Species* as one of the truly great books of all time. Scientific specialists thought differently.

To be sure, plenty of scientific specialists continued to believe in some form of natural selection, but their views on the hows and whys of evolution differed greatly. Some were gradualists, believing that evolution took place over a very long period of time, with incremental changes. Others claimed that in order for evolution to have succeeded this far, there had to have been sudden bursts to accelerate the process. Still others believed in a combination of the two.

One thing that most scientists—whether biologists or paleontologists—agreed upon was that Earth was even older than the most daring of their predecessors had thought. Where it had once been considered extraordinary to say that the world was, perhaps, a billion years old, scientists now generally concurred that it was 4 billion to 5 billion years old and that the universe was more like 16 billion years old. These enormously expanded timelines gave evolutionists more room to maneuver and more reasons to argue, even bicker, for it was much more possible to read all sorts of things into the evolutionary record, if there was that much time involved in the process.

CREATIONISM IN 2009

The year 2009 was also the two hundredth anniversary of the birth of Abraham Lincoln (he and Darwin were born on precisely the same day). Many historians looked back to the births of these nineteenth-century giants to see how far the world had come.

Lincoln was practically raised on the Bible, and it is easy to see how he, had he been introduced to Darwin's theory, would have disagreed with the theory of evolution. On the other hand, Lincoln was a supremely rational, pragmatic person, and one can almost equally envision him accepting the theory over time.

Biblical literalists did not claim Lincoln as an inspiration, and they certainly had no good words for Darwin, but they had almost nowhere to go in 2009. In the United States, most teachers would not argue for the literal biblical story of six days'

In 2001, Kent Hovind, a young earth creationist (one that believes that Earth and the universe are approximately 6,000 years old and professes to have a scientific explanation of the origins of life based on the Bible) built Dinosaur Adventure Land (DAL) in Pensacola, Florida. DAL depicts humans and dinosaurs coexisting and claims to prove that evolution is false. On August 24, 2009, the amusement park was closed until further notice.

creation, or the idea that Earth was only 6,000 years old. What *did* remain was a large number of people for whom there was no contradiction. They could easily conceive of a creator God who set up the universe and allowed it to function through the slow process of evolution.

There the matter might have rested, except for the new hypothesis of intelligent design.

INTELLIGENT DESIGN

Often called "ID," intelligent design was a new hypothesis, dating from the middle part of the 1980s. No one person could claim to have originated the theory or to have started the movement. Instead, it was a hodgepodge that had been worked on by many people. But the hypothesis was both simple and extremely controversial.

Believers in intelligent design claimed that the universe contained too many complex organisms, some going back millions of years, for this to have happened by mere accident. There had to be more at work, and they found the backing for their hypothesis in what they called irreducible complexity.

Irreducible complexity meant that certain organic matter was too inherently complex to have evolved over a long period of time; it had to have begun with something quite complex. This was the cornerstone of the intelligent design hypothesis, and at the beginning of the new century and millennium, intelligent design was gaining strength within the nation at large. Rather few scientists subscribed to it, but those who did were adamant that this was not a clever scheme for reintroducing biblical creationism to the schools: It was an entirely new theory, all on its own.

THE CONTEST

In 2004, a rural Pennsylvania school district introduced the teaching of intelligent design, not as a replacement for Darwinian evolution but as a competing theory. Seven school board members spoke strongly in favor, and a number of families spoke against it. Before long there was a case in federal court, the case of *Kitzmiller v. Dover Area School District*.

Federal Judge John E. Jones gave his ruling in December 2005: "After a searching review of the record and applicable case law, we find that while ID arguments may be true, a proposition on which the Court takes no position, ID is not science."[1]

EXPERTS NOW, EXPERTS THEN

How one wishes that a trial like that of Scopes could occur today and that the scientists would be allowed to testify! Doubtless, they would impress any jury with the weight of their evidence, but there would also be tense moments, because of the wide differences among those who have studied evolution for a lifetime.

Stephen Jay Gould was the most widely read paleontologist of the late twentieth century. Teaching at Harvard and writing on any number of scientific topics, he reached a broad audience. Gould introduced the idea of "punctuated equilibrium," which asserted that evolution usually moves slowly, but that certain parts of the fossil record can only be explained by sharp, sudden moves

(continues)

Stephen Jay Gould (1941–2002) was one of the most influential and widely read writers and lecturers on scientific topics.

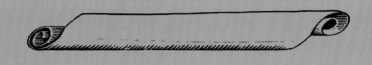

(continued)

forward. Gould was also noted for his rather sarcastic dismissal of the idea of progress. Humans were just one of many branches in the evolutionary tree, and there was no reason to think they represented any grand synthesis. Gould went further, saying that evolution itself probably had no purpose. It simply was the response to stimuli.

Other scientists disagreed. One noted that Gould—hailed by the general public—got very little respect from his academic fellows. No one had a perfect answer to his idea of "punctuated equilibrium," but many thought there was not enough evidence to support it.

One thing the United States lacked in 2009 was a reporter and social commentator with the biting wit of H.L. Mencken. Perhaps no one wanted to don the mantle, as Mencken had often made himself very unpopular, but the fact remains that no journalist since the 1940s has had the kind of influence—for good or ill—that Mencken had at the height of his career.

The era of personalities, clearly, had not ended with Darrow, Bryan, and H.L. Mencken.

Science, as Jones explained, has to be verifiable. Two independent scientists must be able to use the same data and methods to arrive at the same conclusion, and there must be confidence that the experiment could be replicated, time and again. This was the case, he declared, with evolution (whether one called it Darwinian, Neo-Darwinian, or anything else). One hundred and fifty years of looking at geological and pale-ontological evidence had convinced the vast majority of scientists that evolution was an established fact: Plenty of questions still remained as to how it had taken place.

By contrast, intelligent design had failed in one of the major test areas. Articles on the subject had yet to appear in major peer-reviewed journals. Jones, who was a churchgoer, declared that it was not in the purview of the court to say whether intelligent design was true or not—that it might be—but that the court had to rule that it did not fall within the bounds of science. If it was to be taught in the public schools, it would have to be in the area of theology, not of science.

There was yet another test case, however. In the autumn of 2004, Kansas voters returned a state board of education with a narrow majority of Christian fundamentalists. In the spring of 2005, the Kansas Board of Education looked into a similar matter: that of barring Darwin and evolution from its textbooks altogether. The case won only minor attention until *Time* magazine highlighted it in the cover story, "The Evolution Wars," in August of that year. According to *Time*, the conservative-leaning board of education was on the verge of excluding Darwin's theory from new state textbooks. The Board of Education did not go that far, but in October 2005 it voted to instruct schools to teach that evolution was a controversial theory, with plenty of room for disagreement.

The Kansas debate brought more attention than the Board of Education, or the voters, desired, and in 2007 the board revised its guidelines yet again. No longer was it necessary to describe evolution as an unproven theory.

LOOKING FORWARD

And so, in the anniversary year of 2009, a handful of facts remained.

☆ American scientists, perhaps 99 percent of them, believed in evolution.

☆ They often disagreed about the ways evolution had taken place.

☆ The American public was still split on the matter, with a significant number doubting evolution in favor of biblical creation. A Gallup poll conducted in February 2009 showed that 39 percent of Americans believed in evolution, 25 percent did not, and 36 percent had no opinion either way.

☆ There was the new, still small and struggling, hypothesis of intelligent design.

What lessons can be drawn from the Scopes Monkey Trial?

The personalities, and quirks, of prominent people—whether they be Bryan, Darrow, or some future leader—play an important role in events such as the Monkey Trial. There is no way to "rid" the courtroom of them; as one attorney joked during the trial, lawyers are a necessary evil.

The rule of law, as practiced in the United States, still, and for the foreseeable future, relies on the common sense of 12 citizens, selected for the purpose, rather than on the testimony of experts. One can argue that science should be "tried" in the laboratory, in the classroom, and in the presence of one's academic peers, but the fact remains that the taxpayers will have the final say when it comes to what is taught in the schools.

Science has come a very long way since the publication of *The Origin of Species*, and it will doubtless progress further yet. Darwin's seminal publication was the beginning of a great discussion of who human beings are, and where they come from, but it is doubtful that he, or anyone else, will have the last word.

CHRONOLOGY

1859   Charles Darwin's *The Origin of Species* is published.

1871   Darwin's book *The Descent of Man* is published.

1883   *What Social Classes Owe Each Other* by William Graham Sumner, a social Darwinist, is published.

1910–1915   *The Fundamentals,* a set of 90 essays in 12 volumes on the fundamentals of Christianity, is published by the Bible Institute of Los Angeles.

1914   World War I begins.

1917   The United States enters the war.

1918   World War I ends with an Allied victory.

1918–1919   The Spanish influenza epidemic kills millions of people worldwide, including about 600,000 in the United States.

1920   The American Civil Liberties Union (ACLU) is founded. Its mission is "to defend and preserve the individual rights and liberties guaranteed to every person in this country by the Constitution and laws of the United States."

1924   Clarence Darrow, an opponent of capital punishment, defends Nathan Leopold and Richard Loeb in what is called the Leopold-Loeb Trial. It becomes a media spectacle and is one of the first cases to be called the "Trial of the Century."

1925   **March** The Butler Act, which forbids public school teachers to teach evolution, becomes Tennessee law.

April The ACLU announces that it will finance a test case challenging the constitutionality of the Butler Act if it could find a teacher willing to act as a defendant.

May 5 Teacher John T. Scopes is approached by a group of businessmen at Robinson's drugstore and is persuaded to serve as defendant in a trial accusing him of teaching the theory of evolution. Scopes is later indicted and charged with teaching evolution to a high school class on April 7.

July 10 The Scopes Trial begins with jury selection.

July 20 Clarence Darrow is cited for contempt for going too far in questioning the court. Judge John T. Raulston

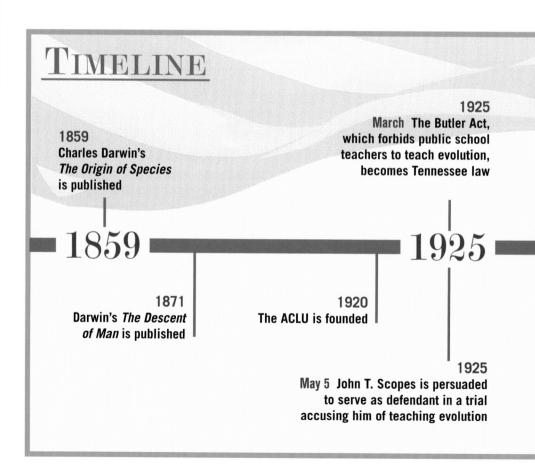

TIMELINE

1859
Charles Darwin's
The Origin of Species
is published

1925
March **The Butler Act,**
which forbids public school
teachers to teach evolution,
becomes Tennessee law

1859   1925

1871
Darwin's *The Descent
of Man* is published

1920
The ACLU is founded

1925
May 5 **John T. Scopes is persuaded**
to serve as defendant in a trial
accusing him of teaching evolution

later accepts his apology and decides to hold the trial on the courthouse lawn. In the afternoon, Darrow calls prosecutor William Jennings Bryan to the witness stand to question him on the Bible. Bryan is caught off guard in the exchange. The next day, Judge Raulston removes his answers from the court records.

July 21 The Scopes Trial ends with conviction and a $100 fine.

July 26 Bryan dies in his sleep.

1953 Graduate student Francis Crick and research fellow James Watson discover DNA (one of two types of molecules that contain genetic instructions used in

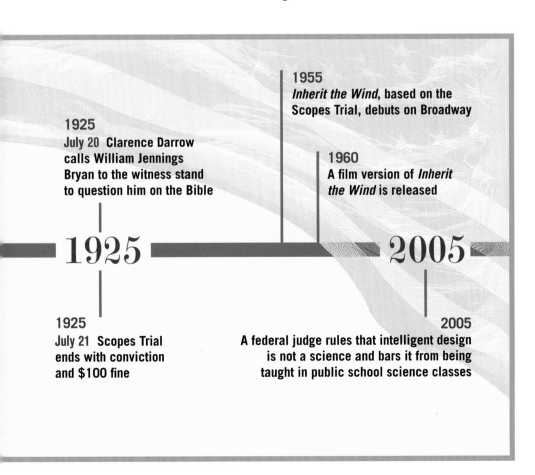

1955
Inherit the Wind, based on the Scopes Trial, debuts on Broadway

1925
July 20 Clarence Darrow calls William Jennings Bryan to the witness stand to question him on the Bible

1960
A film version of *Inherit the Wind* is released

1925

2005

1925
July 21 Scopes Trial ends with conviction and $100 fine

2005
A federal judge rules that intelligent design is not a science and bars it from being taught in public school science classes

the development and function of all humans). This is called the most important biological work of the last 100 years.

1955   *Inherit the Wind*, a fictionalized account of the Scopes Monkey Trial, debuts on Broadway. It is a means to discuss the McCarthy hearings of the 1950s.

1960   *Inherit the Wind* becomes a movie, starring Spencer Tracy, Frederic March, and Gene Kelly, as fictionalized versions of Darrow, Bryan, and H.L. Mencken, respectively. Tracy is nominated for an Academy Award for his portrayal.

2005   In *Kitzmiller v. Dover Area School District*, a group of parents of high school students challenge a public school district in Pennsylvania that requires teachers to present intelligent design in biology classes as an alternative to evolution. Intelligent design is the belief that "certain features of the universe and of living things are best explained by an intelligent cause, not an undirected process such as natural selection." Federal Judge John E. Jones rules that intelligent design is not a science and the school district violated the Constitution. He bars it from being taught in the district's science classes.

NOTES

CHAPTER 2

1. Charles Darwin, *The Descent of Man.* New York: The Modern Library, 1944, 919.
2. Ibid., 919–920.
3. Ibid., 920.
4. George William Hunter, *A Civic Biology: Presented in Problems.* New York: American Book Company, 1914, 195–196.
5. Anne Janette Johnson, *The Scopes "Monkey Trial."* Detroit, Mich.: Omnigraphics, 2007, 274.

CHAPTER 3

1. John T. Scopes and James Presley, *Center of the Storm.* New York: Holt, Rinehart and Winston, 1967, 58.
2. Ibid., 59.
3. Ibid.
4. Ibid.
5. *The Monkey Trial*, The History Channel, DVD.
6. Scopes and Presley, *Center of the Storm*, p. 70.
7. H.L. Mencken, *Prejudices: Second Series.* New York: Alfred A. Knopf, 1920, 136–137.

CHAPTER 4

1. *The Monkey Trial*, The History Channel, 2001.
2. *The World's Most Famous Trial: Tennessee Evolution Case.* Cincinnati: National Book Company, 1925, 11.
3. Ibid., 12.
4. Ibid., 13.
5. Ibid., 14.

6. Ibid.
7. Ibid., 19–20.
8. Ibid., 25.

CHAPTER 5

1. H.L. Mencken, *Prejudices, Fifth Series.* New York: Alfred A. Knopf, 1926, 82–83.
2. *The World's Most Famous Trial*, 48.
3. Ibid., 49.
4. Ibid., 53.
5. Ibid., 58.
6. Edward J. Larson, *Summer for the Gods: The Scopes Trial and America's Continuing Debate over Science and Religion.* Cambridge, Mass: Harvard University Press, 1997, 160.
8. Ibid., 66.
9. Ibid., 74.
10. Ibid., 75.
11. Ibid., 77–78
12. Ibid., 83.

CHAPTER 6

1. *The World's Most Famous Trial*, 108.
2. Ibid., 116.
3. Ibid., 123.
4. Ibid., 126.
5. Ibid., 128.
6. Ibid., 129.
7. Ibid., 137.
8. Ibid., 139.
9. Ibid., 142.

CHAPTER 7

1. *The World's Most Famous Trial*, 154.

2. Ibid., 170.
3. Ibid.
4. Ibid., 172.
5. Ibid., 173.
6. Ibid., 174.
7. Ibid., 183.
8. Ibid., 189.
9. Ibid., 184.
10. Ibid., 185.
11. Scopes and Presley, *Center of the Storm*, 155.
12. *The World's Most Famous Trial*, 187.

CHAPTER 8

1. *The World's Most Famous Trial*, 203.
2. Ibid., 206.
3. Ibid., 206–207.
4. Jerry R. Tompkins, *D-Days at Dayton*.
5. Ibid., 226.

6. Ibid., 284.
7. Ibid., 285.
8. Ibid.
9. Ibid., 287.
10. Ibid.
11. Ibid., 298–299.
12. Ibid., 299.
13. Ibid., 302.
14. Ibid., 304.

CHAPTER 9

1. *The World's Most Famous Trial*, 306.
2. Ibid., 310.
3. Ibid., 313.
4. Mencken, *Prejudices, Fifth Series*, 67.

CHAPTER 10

1. Johnson, *The Scopes Monkey Trial*, 195.

BIBLIOGRAPHY

Darwin, Charles. *The Origin of Species: 150th Anniversary Edition.* New York: Signet Classics, 2003.

———, and Carl Zimmer, editor. *The Descent of Man: Concise Edition.* New York: Plume, 2007.

Johnson, Anne Janette. *The Scopes "Monkey Trial."* Detroit, Mich.: Omnigraphics, 2007.

Larson, Edward J. *Summer for the Gods: The Scopes Trial and America's Continuing Debate over Science and Religion.* Cambridge, Mass.: Harvard University Press, 1997.

McRae, Donald. *The Last Trials of Clarence Darrow.* New York: William Morrow, 2009.

Mencken, H.L. *Prejudices: Fifth Series.* New York: Alfred A. Knopf, 1920, 1926.

Rodgers, Marion Elizabeth. *Mencken: The American Iconoclast.* New York: Oxford University Press, 2005.

Scopes, John T., and James Presley. *Center of the Storm.* New York: Holt, Rinehart and Winston, 1967.

The World's Most Famous Trial: Tennessee Evolution Case. Cincinnati: National Book Company, 1925.

Wallis, Claudia. "The Evolution Wars," *Time* magazine, August 15, 2005.

FURTHER READING

BOOKS

Bryant, Jennifer. *Ringside, 1925: View from the Scopes Trial.* New York: Alfred A. Knopf, 2008.

McRae, Donald. *The Last Trials of Clarence Darrow.* New York: William Morrow, 2009.

Uschan, Michel V. *The Scopes Monkey Trial.* Milwaukee: World Almanac Library, 2005.

WEB SITES

American Civil Liberties Union

http://www.aclu.org/

The home site of the ACLU describes its mission, its history, and its current efforts in the legal sphere.

City of Dayton, Tennessee

http://www.daytontn.net/

The Web site of the city where the famous trial occurred.

Famous Trials in American History

http://www.law.umkc.edu/faculty/projects/ftrials/scopes/scopes. htm

Dozens of important trials are featured in this Web site from the University of Missouri-Kansas City School of Law.

H.L. Mencken Quotes

http://www.lhup.edu/~dsimanek/mencken.htm

Some of the spiciest, and most barbed, of the famous reporter's quotes.

Photo Credits

INDEX

About the Author

SAMUEL WILLARD CROMPTON still remembers his high school biology class, where the emphasis, and controversy, was on genetics rather than evolution. He teaches history at Westfield State College and lives in the Berkshire Hills of his native western Massachusetts. Crompton is the author or editor of many books, including several written for this series.